History of a Glass Family in America

*AN ACCOUNT OF THE DESCENDANTS OF
JOHN GLASSE OF SOMERSET, ENGLAND*

Gene V Glass

Glass Family in America

Cover: A painting from the mid-1800s by Sophia Towne Darrah (1819-1881) depicts the area known as Glass Head, at the entrance to Manchester Harbor, 20 miles north of the center of Boston, Massachusetts.

Copyright © 2016 by Gene V Glass

Dedication

This book is dedicated to the memory of the departed descendants of John Glasse of Taunton, Somerset, England, who braved the dangers of a transatlantic crossing in the early 1600s in search of religious liberty and a safer more prosperous life, who wrested an existence from the forests and rocky hills of Plymouth, Massachusetts, Connecticut, and Vermont, who traveled the Great Lakes region in search of arable land to sustain growing families, who fought in the Civil War for the Union, who followed the expansion of the transcontinental railroad that opened the West, and who labored in the emerging trades of the early 20th Century, so that we, the living descendants of John Glasse can enjoy the safety, comforts, and peace of the 21st Century.

May we, the living, do as well by our descendants.

Glass Family in America

TABLE OF CONTENTS

	Page
INTRODUCTION	1
A BRIEF HISTORY OF A GLASS FAMILY IN AMERICA	5
Note on Ethnicity of the Some of the Glass Family	11
HISTORY OF A GLASS FAMILY IN AMERICA	13
1550 The Glass Family in Somerset, England	13
1637 The Glass Siblings Come to America	16
1740 Some Glass Ancestors Move to Connecticut	32
1770 Migration to Vermont, New York	35
1873 Westward Movement, To Nebraska	54
1950 The Diaspora	82
BRIEF BIOGRAPHIES	115
SELECTED DESCENDANTS OF JOHN GLASSE	146
REFERENCES	168
ACKNOWLEDGMENTS	169
NAME INDEX	172

INTRODUCTION

What follows is a brief and selective account of the descendants of four siblings (three male and one female) who left Taunton, Somerset, England in 1637, in search of a better life in America. Roger, Henry, Amy, and James Glass account for, perhaps, tens of thousands of persons in the United States with the surname Glass. In the 2000 U.S. Census, Glass was the 770th most common surname, and it was used by about 40,000 persons. Persons with the surname Glass in the U.S. generally have English, Irish, Scottish, or Jewish ancestry. The descendants focused on here migrated from England to Massachusetts in the early 1600s, then to Connecticut, Vermont, New York, Michigan, and Nebraska. Other descendants of the three brothers are to be found in Western Illinois, Minnesota, and by the 21st Century, virtually everywhere in the country.

The figure below shows the frequency of the surname Glass, based on the 2000 U.S. Census. The darker the shade of the state, the more numerous are the persons with the Glass surname. What one sees there is the northern Glass families – many related to the Somerset Glass siblings – and the southern Glass families, who may be Scots or Scots-Irish and who likely entered the U.S. through Philadelphia and originally settled in Appalachia and Virginia.

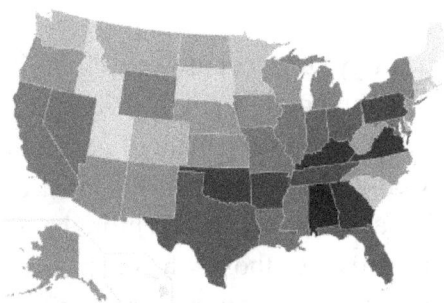

Glass Family in America

This is neither the work of a professional genealogist nor a historian. It is the work of an amateur. Nearly all the information has been obtained through Internet searches and surviving personal records such as correspondence. Professional genealogists would likely not approve of all the methods used in exploring this family's history. Nor do I approve of the occasional display of anal retentiveness by the professionals. Some years ago while corresponding with a professional genealogist, my claim that my great-grandfather migrated from Michigan to Nebraska was challenged for lack of "documentation." My response was that one of the few documents about my family's history in my possession – my own birth certificate – listed my father's place of birth as Friend, Nebraska, a town roughly 300 miles from where he was actually born. At times, the most authoritative documents will be in error. More often, family lore cannot be taken at face value. What you will see, if you persist in reading this account, is that families sometimes create myths, more often, I suspect, for protection than for self-aggrandizement.

All evidence has to be weighed in the scales of probability. Often, the tests of consistency or simple logic will count more heavily in the evaluation of evidence than will documentation, for even documents must be subjected to these same standards. I am no stranger to probabilistic reasoning nor to the evaluation of evidence, and I have done the best I can over hundreds of hours of investigation to present the most reliable account of which I am capable.

The backward trek of every genealogy stops somewhere short of the Garden of Eden. This one comes to an end in the mid-1500s in Somerset, a county in southwest England. In the resulting chain of generations are a couple weak links. The least well-known links in the chain are in Duxbury, Plymouth Colony, Massachusetts, and in Whitingham, Windham, Vermont, in the mid-1700s. For those who wish to follow the succession of generations through the Michigan migration of the Reuben

Glass family, the key to greater confidence lies in the details of the James Glass family of Windham County, Connecticut and Windham County, Vermont, between about 1750 and 1790.

Any "family tree" is a very complex structure. The account presented here spans some 16 generations of the descendants of John Glasse of Taunton, Somerset, England to the recent births of Jackson Paul Glass, Cameron Elizabeth Glass, Caydin Warren Greggs, and Maleah Rene Greggs. I hasten to add, in the interest of celebrating our diversity, that the combined heritage of these three children includes, but is not limited to, England, France, Wales, Scotland, Germany, Scandinavia, Cambodia, Spain, and Meso-America.

If you are drawn to this account out of a desire to find your royal lineage, you may be disappointed. It is not that such connections do not exist; they probably do, though they have not been confidently discovered and reported here. At one point, it appeared that the marriage of a Glass male to a descendant of the Harrington family was the connection of Glass descendants to King Henry I, William the Conqueror, and Charlemagne. However, apparently there were two Benjamin Harringtons in Boston in the 1700s, and DNA testing of known descendants of Henry I has demonstrated that *our* Benjamin Harrington is not *the* Benjamin Harrington. But be not discouraged. The descendants of persons who lived 600 and more years ago are so numerous that you, dear reader, can probably claim royal lineage – we just don't know right now to whom. A few years ago, I was under the misapprehension that we were in fact of the royal Benjamin Harrington line. I announced as much to a friend who got me interested in genealogical research in the 1960s. "Bob, I'm descended from Charlemagne," I reported proudly. "Oh, that's wonderful," replied Bob.

"I think about half the people I know are descendants of Charlemagne," he added wryly.

Rest assured, you are very likely genetically related to royalty. The idea that virtually anyone with a European ancestor descends from English royalty is difficult to grasp. However, it has been proven to be true by Joseph Chang, a statistician at Yale University. Go back forty generations, to about the Norman Conquest in 1066, and each of us has more than a trillion ancestors – a number greater than the total number of persons in human history. So, yes, you are genetically related to Charlemagne, King of the Franks who united all of Western Europe in the late 700s. And my friend Bob underestimated the number of his friends who likewise are descendants of Charlemagne; virtually all of them are. However, the number of genes in your DNA that existed in Charlemagne's DNA is infinitesimal. The actual important connection between you and the King of the Franks is that you and he both eat beef (unless you are a vegetarian), drink wine, and read text with Roman letters; and these inheritances are more important than a scintilla of DNA.

At each generation, at the very least, these descendants multiply by a power of 2, and across 16 generations, the tree encompasses as a minimum more than 65,000 persons. That only a couple hundred persons are mentioned here reflects the fact that the person writing the account occupies a particular position of interest to him and those persons close to him, primarily his siblings and their descendants. If you feel that persons important to you are not represented here, then I fear that the only solution is to write your own family history. Never before have the resources to do so been so readily at hand.

One or two previously written genealogies have been helpful in producing this account. They are identified in the REFERENCES.

      Gene V Glass, September 11, 2016, Boulder, Colorado

A BRIEF HISTORY OF A
GLASS FAMILY IN AMERICA

The bulk of what follows here is a listing of names, dates, and facts about the descendants of a family with the surname Glass(e) who lived in Somerset, England in the 1500s. At least four children of that family migrated to the Boston area in 1637.[1] If you are reading these sentences, it is likely that you are a descendant of that family or married into that family or otherwise have some very close connection to the John Glasse family of Taunton, Somerset, England. Otherwise, I can't imagine why you would be interested.

The number of descendants of those four siblings who emigrated to America must be counted in the tens of thousands, if not more. The probability is considerable that someone with the surname Glass living in Massachusetts, Vermont, western New York State, Michigan, or Nebraska in the mid-1900s is a descendant of John Glasse. There are probably two other sources of the Glass surname in America. (In the 1950 Census, the surname Glass appeared about 50,000 times.) A family of Glasses appears in the South some two to three hundred years ago. That family counts among its descendants a Secretary of the Treasury under Woodrow Wilson[2] and a number of newspaper publishers in Virginia. Another source of the Glass surname in America is that it was frequently chosen by Ashkenazi Jews who arrived in America around

---

[1] The year 1637 is 30 years after the establishment of Jamestown in Virginia, the first successful European colony to be founded in North America. It is estimated that between 1630 and 1640, approximately 18,000 English men and women migrated to New England, 13,000 of them to Massachusetts.

[2] Carter Glass is one of the authors of the Glass-Steagall Act, a very important piece of legislation that established a "firewall" between the commercial banking and the investment banking industries. The repeal of Glass-Steagall during the Bill Clinton administration directly led to the financial crisis of 2008.

1900. The modernist composer Philip Glass is among the descendants of these immigrants.

Because of the practice of wives taking the surname of their husbands, many branches of the Glass family tree are untraceable. The complete list of surnames arising from the marriages of Glass women would number several hundred. Several surnames other than Glass which appear in this account follow: Bumpas, Willis, Holman (Homan), Hunt, Rogers, Linnell, Tinkham, Osband, Frost, Spence, Ryd, Martinez, Sawvel, Cornelison, Richards, Hoover, Ath-Spence, Greggs. Further investigation of these surnames will add to the Glass family genealogy.

In the next several paragraphs, I will attempt to sketch a brief history of the Glass family for those who have no appetite to wade through the many pages of facts and figures.

The earliest record of our Glass family locates them in Taunton, Somerset, England, in about 1550. John Glasse may have been of Welsh descent, but that is merely a guess. In Welsh, the word "glass" meant "green." The Glasse family would have been poor. Their lives would have been closely connected to the church St. Mary Magdalene in Taunton. Religion in England at that time was in turmoil. Henry VIII created the Church of England in 1530 because the Pope refused to grant him an annulment from his wife who could not bear him a son. The Church retained too much of the ritual of the Catholic Church in the opinion of the Puritans. The Glasse family were likely Puritans.

John Glasse had a son whom he named James – a name that was to recur frequently among descendants. James married a Mary Cogan and they had many children. (Mary, incidentally, was from a Welsh family whose pedigree extends back to the Norman Conquest of the Anglo Saxons in 1066.) Among these children were Henry, James, Roger, and Amy.

England in 1640 was not a safe place for young men. Civil War[3] would break out in two years. The four Glass siblings arrived in the Boston area in about 1637, some 17 years after the landing of the Pilgrims at Plymouth Rock.

The three brothers were indentured servants to relatives – Cogans. Once free of that obligation, they may have made their living as fishermen. As one genealogist has concluded: "we can be nearly certain that Henry, Richard (Sr.), and Richard (Jr.) [Henry's son and grandson] were New England mariners, that is, sailors and fishermen, all seemingly humble in origin, at least two of them having been apprenticed." (Shaver, *From Great Britain to Western Illinois: A Glass-Cone-Smith Genealogical Sequel to Plant a Tree by Alan E. Shaver*, p. 6)

Roger eventually appears in the Duxbury, Plymouth, Massachusetts area, where he served in some capacity as a colleague of Miles Standish[4] and John Alden, of Longfellow literature fame. Henry resided in the area near the mouth of Manchester Harbor, just a few miles north of Boston. His son and grandson – both named Richard – continued to reside there, the latter having built a house in 1666 at a rocky promontory still known as Glass Head.

Henry's great-grandson Richard, moved to Connecticut where he became one of the founders of the Westminster Society of Congregationalists. Richard Glass fathered several children. Two of the children were Rufus and Samuel. Both brothers moved to Wells, Vermont, after the Revolutionary War. Rufus and William Cowdry married sisters: Huldah and Rebecca Fuller. Rebecca and William had a

---

[3] The English Civil War (1642–1651) was a series of battles between Parliamentarians ("Roundheads") and Royalists ("Cavaliers") over the manner of its government.
[4] The Standish line joined the Glass line in 1800 when a descendant of Miles's married an Amasa Glass in Duxbury.

son named Oliver Cowdry. The Glass and Cowdry families lived a mile apart in Wells. Oliver lived with the Rufus Glass family for about six years as a child and young man.

One historian of Wells has suggested that after Rebecca's death two-year old Oliver went to live with his aunt Huldah Glass, his mother's older sister. Various records indicate that Oliver may have lived with the Glass family for at least two extended periods, first from 1809 to 1813 and again between 1820 and 1822. The 1810 census record for William Cowdry, for example, lists only one male child under ten although Lyman and Oliver were both in that age bracket. Furthermore the Glass census record for 1810 lists two boys under ten, even though the Glass boys were all over ten. Oliver's living with the Glass family would be consistent with both census reports.[5]

Oliver later was one of three amanuenses (stenographers, in effect) who wrote down the Book of Mormon as it was translated behind a curtain by Joseph Smith, who had been born in nearby Sharon, Vermont. Oliver had followed Joseph Smith to New York State, having befriended Smith growing up in Vermont. Oliver was the first person baptized into the LDS church.

It was during the Revolutionary War that the myth originated that the Glasses were Scottish, or Scots-Irish. This false lead thwarted genealogical research for several years. It was understandable that an English family, like the Glasses, would wish to have others think that they were not English, since English Colonists were often badly treated, having their property confiscated or worse.

It is often asked whether the Glass family history includes the famous frontiersman Hugh Glass whose life included significant episodes in

---

[5] Morris, Larry E. (2000) Oliver Cowdery's Vermont years and the origins of Mormonism.
https://ojs.lib.byu.edu/spc/index.php/BYUStudies/article/viewFile/6631/6280

Nebraska. Hugh Glass was the subject of a movie, The Revenant, released in 2015 starring Leonardo DiCaprio as the main character. Hugh Glass was born in Pennsylvania in about 1780 of Scots-Irish parents. He is not related to the many Glasses in this history.

Among Anthony Richard Glass's children was James Glass, who was born in 1744. James fathered about eight children by two wives. With his first wife, Hannah Sufford, he fathered Parthenia and Philetus. Little is known about Parthenia, but Philetus's line is fairly well known. Philetus eventually settled in Erie, Pennsylvania, where he built a foundry. He was identified as an important part of the Underground Railroad that was the principal organization working to transport runaway slaves to Canada. Philetus named one of his sons Philetus, and descendants of this line are numerous in the area of western Pennsylvania, particularly the city of Erie.

James's second wife was Ruth Bassett. Among their children was Reuben Glass who was born in 1787. With the appearance of Reuben, all doubt about the lineage of the Glass family that later emerges in Nebraska is erased. Reuben was born in Vermont, lived most of his early life in New York State, and migrated to Michigan in 1833. He settled in the village of Nankin, in an area that is today a western suburb of Detroit. Reuben is buried in the Newburgh cemetery near Livonia, Michigan.

Among the several children of Reuben and Ana Wells was Zenas W. Glass.[6] Zenas was born in New York and spent most of his early years there, but by 1835, he had migrated to Nankin near Detroit. There he met a young woman named Sarah Jane Ferris, who had left her father's

---

[6] The name "Zenas" appears among the descendants of Anthony Richard Glass. Ezekiel Glass named a son Zenas Thomas Glass. This further strengthens the argument that Zenas W is descended from Anthony Richard, hence, from the Henry Glass line.

home on the western shore of Lake Champlain, New York, on account of disagreements with her father's second wife. Sarah probably traveled part of the distance from Westport, NY, to Detroit on the newly created Erie Canal.

Zenas and Sarah were married and had several children. He died in 1857 before the Civil War, and Sarah remarried Isaac F. Perrin,[7] a mill owner in a tiny village known as Perrinsville. Isaac and Sarah's marriage was very brief; he died on July 5, 1867, and Sarah found herself a widow again. Shortly thereafter she married her third husband, James Stephenson. He died in 1904 in Michigan. Thus, did Sarah outlive three husbands. In about 1905, her son Edwin Zenis traveled from Nebraska to Michigan to relocate her to Lincoln.

Among Zenas and Sarah's children were Milton, Reuben, and Edwin. Milton served in the Civil War, was wounded, transported to a hospital in Baltimore, and died shortly thereafter. He kept a diary for about six months prior to being wounded; that diary is, at this time, in the possession of Jason Scott Glass (Generation 15).

Edwin Zenas Glass and his brother Reuben E. Glass migrated to Nebraska in about 1875. Reuben settled near Broken Bow, Nebraska, where he farmed; he left no descendants. Edwin returned briefly to Michigan to marry Eva Gillett and bring her back to Nebraska. He worked as an engineer on the railroad and was stationed in Lincoln, Nebraska. Their only child was born in 1883, and they named him Edwin Origen Glass after his father and an uncle, Origen Frost.

Edwin Origen Glass married Nora Ellen Jones, a Welsh young lady, on the Nebraska prairie in the early 1900s; they had six children – five sons and a daughter who died young. Among their children was Edwin Orville Glass – known all his life as Orville. Orville married Grace

---

[7] Isaac F. Perrin was a descendant of John Peryns, who was born on 1380 in Somerset, England.

Virginia Lintt, and their three children were named Edwin Gordon, Ellen Gay, and Gene V. If you are reading these sentences with any degree of interest whatsoever, several of the names in this paragraph will be familiar to you, and you will need no further introduction to the Glass family.

Note on Ethnicity of the Some of the Glass Family

Modern DNA analysis has made possible the tracing of a person's genetic ancestors. It is possible from saliva samples to determine where an individual's ancestors came from some hundreds and even thousands of years ago. In the summer of 2016, your author, Gene V Glass, had his saliva sample analyzed at dna.ancestry.com. The results should be of interest to many of the descendants of Reuben Glass (born 1787 in Vermont), who would be anywhere from direct descendants to 4th or 5th cousins of the target person, GVG.

In the final analysis, the genetic background of many of the Glass family is quite typical of persons descended from inhabitants of England and New England. The vast majority of genes derive from the early inhabitants of Western Europe, Ireland, and Scandinavia. Add to this mixture, approximately 10% Italian ancestry and you have a virtual history of the island now named Great Britain.

Europe West	32%
Ireland	31%
Scandinavia	23%
Italy/Greece	9%
Iberian Peninsula	2%
Finland/Northwest Russia	< 1%
European Jewish	< 1%
Great Britain	< 1%

The Romans occupied modern day Great Britain from about 55 BCE (Before the Common Era) to 410 CE (Common Era). The Romans under Julius Caesar invaded the British Isles in 55 BCE and for the next half millennium left many traces, cultural as well as genetic. The roman occupation likely accounts for the 9% Italian traces in the genes of the present-day Glass family.

The 31% Irish component of the Glass family genes may have arisen from two sources. Dating from about 750 BCE to 12 BCE, the Celts were the most powerful people in central and northern Europe. Many Celtic tribes spread their culture and language from the British Isles in the west to the Ukraine in the east. The modern day Irish and Welsh carry large concentrations of Celtic genes. As will be seen later in this account of the Glass family, there was frequent inter-mingling of Glass ancestors with the Welsh of southwestern England.

The strong presence of Western Europe in the Glass family genealogy reflects the history of England from the departure of the Romans in 410 CE until the arrival of the Normans from western France in 1066. Although the Romans fought off numerous attempts to invade England by the Saxons of modern day Germany, shortly after the Roman departure in the mid-5th century the Saxons took control of vast regions of the British Isles. Frequent attempts at invasion by the Vikings beginning in about 800 CE probably account for the strong presence of Scandinavian genes in the Glass family gene pool. And finally, the Norman invasion in 1066 brought another wave of Western European genes into play.

Until the mid-20th century, the analysis of the Glass family ethnicity is unremarkably like that of most descendants of ancestors who populated the British Isles for more than two millennia. But things began to change radically thereafter. Some 16th generation descendants combine the genetic background of the peoples of all of the ethnicities already mentioned plus those of Spain, Meso-America, and Cambodia.

History of a Glass Family in America

1550 The Glass Family in Somerset, England

It is not known whether the origins of the Glasse family were Saxon, Norman or Welsh, or even some other peoples. One speculation is that the Glasse line descended from inhabitants of Wales. In Welsh, the word Glass means "green." However, it is beyond dispute that the Glass families that were numerous in Massachusetts as early as mid-1600s had arrived in America from Taunton, Somerset, England. The myth that the Glass family in America is Scottish or Scots-Irish was likely created during the Revolutionary War as a protection against suspicion or even violence.

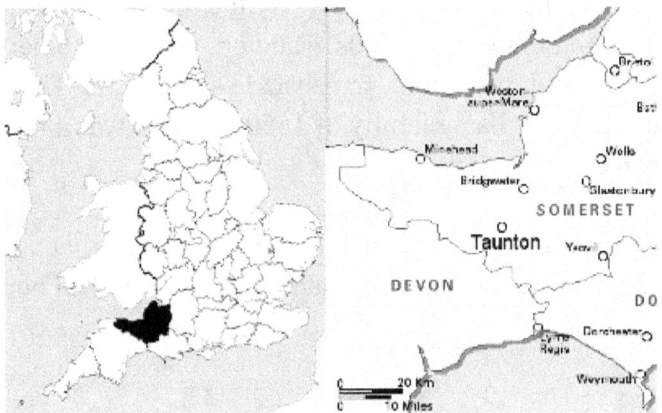

JOHN GLASSE
(About 1535 – Unknown)
GENERATION 0

John Glasse, born in about 1535, is frequently mentioned in family trees without any real documentation. Some of these sources list his date of death as 1590, which is known to be the death date of John Glasse of Taunton who was born in 1555. This John Glasse of Generation 0 may be a fiction, created to push the family genealogy where it cannot safely go.

Glass Family in America

JOHN GLASSE
(About 1561 – 1590)
GENERATION 1

All that is known is that John Glasse, son of John Glasse, resided in the town of Taunton in the county of Somerset in England in the middle of the 16th Century. He undoubtedly attended the church of St. Mary Magdalene. He was very likely a Puritan. At the time, the Puritans were rebelling against the Church of England – created by Henry VIII in 1530 – on account of the presence of too much Catholic ritual. The Puritans sought to purify the Church of these old observances.

Taunton has a history that goes back at least 1000 years before the appearance of John Glasse and his family. By the time John was raising his family in Taunton in the mid-1500s, Taunton, and many other towns and villages in England, were poor, ramshackle settlements. There is little possibility that the Glasse family of 1550 Taunton was a family of significant means.

Church records show the marriage of John to Johane (Joan) Dixon on July 6, 1579. John and Joan had a son named James who was born in about 1590.

JAMES GLASS
(About 1590 – 1638; < John Glasse[8])
GENERATION 2

James's date of birth can only be guessed to have been about 1590, the same year in which his father may have died. It is known from records of St. Mary Magdalene church in Taunton that he married Mary Cogan

---

[8] The notation " James < John " means that James is descended from John. Later, " Eva Ann < Edwin Origen < Edwin Zenis < Zenas " can be read as "Eva Ann, daughter of Edwin Origen, who is son of Edwin Zenis, who is the son of Zenas."

(See BRIEF BIOGRAPHIES, p. 115) on June 24, 1612 or 1613.[9] He died on February 22, 1638, and is presumably buried in Taunton.

James and Mary had 12 children, all born in Taunton.
1. Henry Glass, born about August 1614, Taunton; died young.
2. Mary Glass, born about 1617, Taunton.
3. Amy Glass, born 1618, Taunton; died before 24 January 1648/9 (Age 31) in America.
4. James Glass, born in 1620 in Taunton; died September 3, 1652; died in America.
5. Roger Glass, born 1623, Taunton; died August 27, 1692, Duxbury, MA (Age 69) in America.
6. Henry Glass, born 1624, Taunton; died in America.
7. Joan Glass, born about 1626, Taunton, died July 1627 (Age ~ 1).
8. (A daugher) Glass, died October 1628, Taunton.
9. Joane Glass, born 1629, Taunton; died Apr/May 1640 (Age 11).
10. Richard Glass, born 1616, died August 1629, Taunton.
11. Peter Glass, born 1631, Taunton, died August 1637 (Age 6).
12. Thamazen Glass, born about 1634; died in 1637, Taunton.

It appears that perhaps all of the Glass siblings who survived childhood emigrated to America at the same time.

The Mystery of Lady Mary Glass

Several Glass family genealogists identify a woman known as Mary Glass, daughter of James Glass of Taunton, Somerset, who married a Sir John Henry Maynard, and died in London in 1693. This misattribution is probably the result of enthusiasm to find at least one scrap of nobility in the known

---

[9] Ambiguity in dating events in history usually stems from decisions of those creating the earliest record to use either the Julian or the Gregorian calendar.

Glass Family in America

Glass line. Unfortunately, it is at odds with the facts. James Glass of Taunton died in 1638, and although he had a daughter named Mary, Lady Mary Glass, wife of Sir John Henry Maynard, was born in 1650. There may well be some nobility in the Glass lineage buried far back in history – as there is for most persons of western European ancestry – but we can be confident that it does not involve Lady Mary Glass of 17th century London.

1637 The Glass Siblings Come to America

Four Glass siblings – Amy, James, Roger, and Henry – arrived in America in 1637 aboard the ship Speedwell. They undoubtedly landed somewhere near present-day Boston. The Speedwell was a sister ship of the Mayflower in 1620 and left England with passengers who later came to be known as the Pilgrims. The Speedwell developed a leak; both ships returned to shore, and the passengers were transferred to the Mayflower. (The Speedwell had earlier been named the Swiftsure; it was built in 1577 and participated in the defeat of the Spanish Armada.)

The traversing of the Atlantic by ship in the 1600s was treacherous. The crossing of the Mayflower in 1620 took more than two months; and though it was headed for Virginia, it landed hundreds of miles off course in Plymouth.

AMY GLASS
(1618 – 1648 ; < James Glass < John Glasse)
GENERATION 3

Amy Glass was born to James Glass and Mary (Cogan) Glass on December 10, 1618, in Taunton, Somerset, England. She immigrated to America with siblings James, Henry, and Roger in 1637. She settled in Plymouth, Massachusetts, and married Richard Willis on October 11, 1639, in East Bridgewater. Richard Willis was also born in Taunton. Richard's known lineage goes back to Edward Willis, who was born in 1478, in the Warwickshire area. He is listed as a "Mayflower descendant" in various histories of New England families. In *History of the Early Settlement of Bridgewater in Plymouth County* by Nahum Mitchell, the following sentence appears: "There was a Richard Willis, servant of John Barnes, transferred by consent to Thomas Prince 1634, m. Amy Glasse 1639."

Amy's second marriage in 1645 was to Edward Holman (or Homan). Edward had arrived in America in 1623, three years after the Mayflower, on a ship named the Anne. Amy bore Edward a son, named Edward as well, in 1647. She died at Plymouth on January 24, 1649.

The book *New England, The Great Migration and The Great Migration Begins, 1620 – 1635* gives some indication of the social status of Edward Holman, and by implication, of Amy Glass, his wife. "Edward Holman clearly existed on the fringes of Plymouth society. He was fined on various occasions for drunkenness and Sabbath-breaking, and was also brought before the court on 7 December 1641 to answer for taking items from a shipwreck, which should have been reported to the authorities." (p. 298)

Glass Family in America

JAMES GLASS
(About 1620 – 1652 ; < James Glasse < John Glasse)
GENERATION 3

James was born in about 1620, at Taunton, Somerset, England. His baptism is not recorded there, but it is believed he was the son of James and Mary (Cogan) Glass, one of 12 children.

James came to Massachusetts as a servant to his uncle Henry Cogan in 1637 on the Speedwell, with three siblings: Amy, Roger, and Henry. His indebtedness probably changed hands a couple of times between 1637 and 1639. On February 13, 1639/40, James Barnes of Barnstable transferred the five-year contract of his servant James Glass to Manasseh Kempton. James Glass was on the 1643 Plymouth Colony list of men able to bear arms.

On October 31, 1645, James married Mary Elizabeth Pontus (see BRIEF BIOGRAPHIES, starting on page 115) in Plymouth, Massachusetts. Mary Pontus was born on October 15, 1622, in the city of Leyden in the Netherlands. The Pilgrims left England seeking religious freedom and first migrated to the Netherlands. Eventually finding matters no better there, they returned to England and prepared for their migration to America. This accounts for Mary's birth in Leyden. Mary died on February 3, 1690, in Plymouth. Mary's mother was Wybra Hansen, a name that James and Mary later conferred on one of their daughters. Wybra was a native of the Netherlands. Mary's father was William Pontus, who was born in Dover, Kent, England, in 1586.

James and Mary Elizabeth Pontus had four daughters:
1. Hannah was born June 2, 1647, and died in 1648.
2. Wybra born August 9, 1649, married Joseph Bumpas.
3. Hannah born December 24, 1651, Plymouth, married Isaac Billington before1675 and died August 30, 1704. Isaac's grandfather, John Billington, was a *Mayflower* passenger.

Hannah and Isaac had one daughter, Lydia, born in 1677, who died in 1716. Lydia married a man named John Washburn in 1698 in Plymouth. No other children of Hannah and Isaac are known. The Washburn line is very long and well documented.
4. Mary born after September 3, 1652, after the death of her father, married Samuel Hunt.

James died at sea in a storm near Plymouth Harbor on September 3, 1652. His father-in-law, William Pontus, named him executor of his estate in his 1650 will, but it is unlikely he served because the inventory was filed February 20, 1652/3 after James died at sea. Mary was the eldest daughter of William Pontus and received his homestead and land at Plymouth. She later married Phillip Delano.

The inventory of the estate of James Glass(e) was taken February 20, 1652 (perhaps 1652/53) and exhibited to the court on March 4, 1652/3 on the oath of Mary Glasse widow. It includes two cows, a steer, a sow, various furniture and household items, a fowling piece, a beer barrel, tools, linens, clothing, and books. He was owed more than five pounds from John Barnes and owned a parcel of land he bought from Samuel Dunham worth five pounds. The inventory totaled more than 32 pounds. The inventory was taken by John Donham Senior and Ephraim Morton.

ROGER GLASS
(1623 – 1692 ; < James Glasse < John Glasse)
GENERATION 3

Roger was born to James Glass and Mary Cogan on August 7, 1623, at Taunton, Somerset, England. Mary Cogan's family played a role in the emigration of Roger and his siblings Henry, James, and Amy Glass to Massachusetts in 1637. The emigration of the four Glass siblings from Somerset was probably due more to economic circumstances than anything having to do with religion. From Roger and Henry have descended many of the persons with the surname Glass in America.[10]

Roger and his brothers, James and Henry, were indentured servants to those who financed their passage to America. He encountered problems after arrival in America, however, for he was released from servitude by the Court when they determined that his master, John Crocker, was mistreating him. In 1640, Roger went to the household of John Whetcomb of Scituate. Whetcomb was the husband of Roger's aunt, Frances Cogan.

> Forasmuch as John Crocker, of Scituate, is proved to have corrected his servant boy, Roger Glass, in a most extreme & barbarous manner, the Court upon due consideration has taken the said Roger Glass from the said John Crocker, and placed him with John Whetcombe, which is six years from the fourteenth of June next; the said John Whetcombe paying the said John Crocker three pounds, deducting five shillings for his charges, & the said Crocker to deliver up his clothes to the said Whetcombe.

Records show that Roger married Mary Launder in Somerset, England, in 1643, and that they were remarried in Massachusetts in 1650. He must have returned to Somerset to wed Mary. Such returns were not uncommon among the colonists in the 17th Century.

It appears possible that Roger and his brother James early moved to Duxbury, Massachusetts, since it is recorded that James Glass of

---

[10] Two other families contributed offspring with the surname Glass. One family, Irish in nationality, that settled in Virginia and counts among its descendants Carter Glass who was Secretary of the Treasury under Woodrow Wilson, and a later arriving Scots-Irish family named Glass. Neither family is related to the Glass family recorded here.

Glass Family in America

Duxbury, Massachusetts, married Mary Pontus on October 31, 1645 and died when lost at sea at age 32 in 1652.

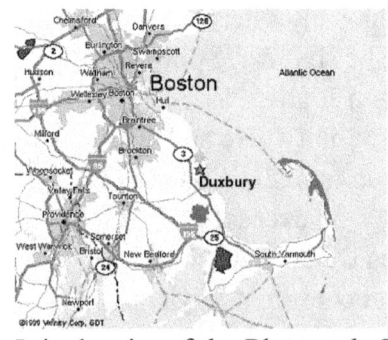

Duxbury is in Plymouth County, about 30 miles south of Boston on the north edge of Cape Cod. Interestingly, it lies about 15 miles east of the town of Taunton, Massachusetts, underlining the close connection between this region of Massachusetts and the town in England from which the Glass siblings emigrated. It is the site of the Plymouth Colony that was established in 1632 by a group that included John Alden and Capt. Miles Standish, both of whom were memorialized by Longfellow in the 1858 poem entitled *The Courtship of Miles Standish*. The history of Duxbury, which includes several references to Roger Glass and his descendants, is entitled *History of the Town of Duxbury, Massachusetts: With Genealogical Registers*, published in 1849 by Justin Winsor. In 2015, it was available on the Internet at https://archive.org/details/historyoftownofd00wins. Roger was identified as one of a group of surveyors of roads in Duxbury in 1669.

Roger lived at Hound's Ditch, which he bought from Constant Southworth in 1657, and he died in Duxbury in 1692. He named five children in his will, written in 1690: sons James (a weaver) and John, and daughters Amey Dwelley, Mary Dwelley and Elizabeth. There are hundreds of persons in the Duxbury, Massachusetts, area with the surname Glass who probably all descended from Roger Glass. Roger was also an apprentice/servant.

Roger Glass left a will written in 1690.
    Will of Roger Glass
    I being old and not knowing ye day of my death, dated
    September 2, 1690. To son James, 20s; to day. Amy Dwelley,

21

10s besides what she hath already; to day. Mary Dwelley, idem; to day. Elizabeth Glass, one cow, one heifer of a year old and four ewe sheep; to son John and to my wife house and lands and rest moveable estate, which after her decease shall all go to son John. If she marry, she shall have only a widow's dowry, and the rest shall be son John's. Wife and son John to be executors. Witnessed by John Soule and Thomas Delano,[11] who made oath to the same, Jan. 14, 1692-3. Inventory of estate of Roger Glass "Who deceased the 7th day of August 1692", taken by Thomas Delano and John Glass August 29, 1692 and presented at court by Mary Glass, widow of Roger, Sept. 21, 1692. Amount, £89..06..11.

It is fairly well documented that James Glass was said to have perished in a "bootless expedition" against Quebec in 1690.[12]

---

[11] Frequent references to a Delano surname are found in the history of the Glass family of Duxbury. These persons are likely to be ancestors of Franklin Delano Roosevelt, through his mother's line.

[12] From Wikipedia: The Battle of Quebec was fought in October 1690 between the colonies of New France and Massachusetts Bay. Following the capture of Port Royal in Acadia, during King William's War, the New Englanders hoped to seize Montreal and Quebec itself, the capital of New France. The loss of the Acadian fort shocked the Canadians, and Governor-General Louis de Buade de Frontenac ordered the immediate preparation of the city for siege. When the envoys delivered the terms of surrender, the Governor-General famously declared that his only reply would be by "the mouth of my cannons." Major John Walley led the invading army, which landed at Beauport in the Basin of Quebec. However, the militia on the shore were constantly harassed by Canadian militia until their retreat, while the expedition's ships, commanded by Sir William Phips, were nearly destroyed by cannon volleys from the top of the city. Both sides learned from the battle: the French improved the city's defences, while the New Englanders realized they needed more artillery and better support from England to take the city.

HENRY GLASS
(1624 – ?; < James < John)
GENERATION 3

Henry Glass was born to James Glass and Mary Cogan in about 1624 in Taunton, Somerset, England. Henry is very likely the progenitor of the Glass family line that can be traced from Boston to Connecticut and eventually to Vermont, New York, Michigan, and Nebraska. Henry arrived in America with three of his siblings – James, Roger, and Amy – in about 1637. Henry was apprenticed to Henry Cogan, a brother of his mother's. This service provided the cost of his passage to America, and obliged him to several years' service to his master. His apprenticeship was sold a couple of times to other individuals. In 1644, he was servant to Giles Rickard of Plymouth. By 1645, he was free of his apprenticeship and employed as a mariner and fisherman. The date and place of his death are not known, though some sources list Duxbury, Plymouth, Massachusetts, which is known to be where his brother Roger[13] settled.

Henry is likely to have left at least one descendant, Richard, born sometime after 1645. Henry had a sibling in England who was named Richard and who died young. He may have named his own son in honor of his deceased brother.

WYBRA GLASS (1649 – 1711; < James Glass < James Glasse < John Glasse)
GENERATION 4

Wybra was born to James Glass and Mary Pontus on August 9, 1649, in the city of Barnstable, Barnstable County, Massachusetts. She died on

---

[13] Roger appears in records of court cases thus: "March 5, 1655/6, Roger Glasse complained against Thomas Bonney for denying to pay him for carrying some things 'into the bay,' the jury finding for the plaintiff."

Glass Family in America

December 29, 1711, in Middleboro, Plymouth, Massachusetts. Wybra married Joseph Bumpas, in about 1668. Wybra and Joseph had eight children: Lydia (1669 - 1770), Wybra (1670 - 1698), Joseph (1674 - 1716), Rebecca (1677 - 1711), James (1679 - 1750), Penelope (1681 - unknown), Mary (1682 - 1717), and Mehitable (1691 - 1749).

Joseph Bumpas (Jr.) married Mary Ford in Middleboro, and they had five children. Penelope Bumpas married Richard Everson and had at least one son whom they named after his father. Wybra, daughter of Wybra and Joseph, married John Washburn. Rebecca married Edward Rose; and Mary married Joseph Benson, and later married William Bassett. The eight children of Wybra and Joseph account for an enormous number of descendants living today, and they cannot be followed here. However, the Joseph (Jr.) Bumpas line is followed through a few generations in what follows later.

HANNAH GLASS (1651 – 1704; < James Glass < James Glasse < John Glasse)
GENERATION 4

Hannah was born on December 24, 1651, in Plymouth. She married Isaac Billington before 1675 and died on August 30, 1704. Isaac's grandfather, John Billington, was a *Mayflower* passenger. Hannah and Isaac had two daughters, Lydia and Eleanor.

MARY (GLASS) HUNT
(1652 – 1707; < James Glass < James Glasse < John Glasse)
GENERATION 4

Mary was born in 1652 in Plymouth County. She was wed to Samuel Hunt (1640 – 1707) in about 1672. Mary and Samuel bore six or seven children: Thomas Hunt, Mary Hunt, John Hunt, Elizabeth, Martha, Samuel. Mary died on February 22, 1712, in Duxbury, Plymouth County,

Massachusetts. The younger Mary Hunt married a man named Jacob Burgess, and they had six children. So the line goes on.

RICHARD WILLIS
(1645 – 1687; < Amy (Glass) Willis < James Glasse < John Glasse)
GENERATION 4

Richard Willis (Jr.) is the son of Amy Glass and Richard Willis. He was born and died in Plymouth, Massachusetts. On December 28, 1670, he married Patience Bonham in Plymouth. Patience's father, George, was born in about 1604 in either the Netherlands or England. Richard and Patience had a daughter whom they named Ruhammah Ammi Willis. The child's middle name is obviously either a variation on her grandmother's name or an approximate spelling of the same.

RICHARD GLASS (Sr.)
(About 1655 –   ; < Henry < James < John)
GENERATION 4

Since Richard, son of Henry, is known to have fathered a son also named Richard, we should refer to the former as Richard (Sr.) and the latter as Richard (Jr.), though undoubtedly they were not so known in their time. Richard (Sr.) has a probable date of birth about 1655. He married Elizabeth Fox of Manchester and had three children: Mary (born October 27, 1684), Joane (born November 13, 1686), and Richard (born March 15, 1687 at Marblehead, MA).

Richard (Sr.) built a dwelling which would be known as Glass Head at the entrance to Manchester Harbor in about 1675. Manchester Harbor is approximately 20 miles north of the center of present-day Boston. Modern maps still identify the rocky promontory at the entrance to the harbor as Glass Head. Glass Head was a key lookout for movements of British ships during the Revolutionary War.

Richard (Sr.) was a mariner and fisherman. He probably maintained two houses, one at Marblehead and the other in Maine in connection with his occupation of fisherman. The *Genealogical Guide to the Early Settlers of America* reports that "Richard Glass of Pemaquid took the oath of fidelity in 1674; was of Manchester, 1686." As mentioned above, Richard built a house at what came to be known as Glass Head. It is also possible that he acquired a house by marriage to Elizabeth Fox. Documents at the Marblehead Museum report that "Nicholas Fox of Marblehead, fisherman, June 26, 1669. Mr. Fox built a house upon the lot, and died before Aug. 13, 1683, possessed of the estate. His widow Elizabeth married, secondly, Richard Glass of Marblehead, mariner, and she, as administratrix of the estate of Mr. Fox, for forty-three pounds, conveyed the house and lot to Samuel Russell of Marblehead, mariner, Oct. 1, 1684. Apparently Mr. Russell removed the house about 1710."

Richard surely served in some version of a colonies militia, for he was punished for having defamed a colleague, Erasmus James, by having to recite the following in front of his unit at Marblehead:

Glass Family in America

> I, Richard Glass do hereby before God and his people here assembled owne and confesse that I have in my words, calling Erasmus James, cheating rogue, one dyde rogue, one dyde dog; sinned against God and wickedly abused the said James, of whom I had no reason to say, and do from my heart beg pardon of God, and of said James, whom I have justly offended in my words, hopeing to be hereafter more watchfull over the rashness of my heart and tongue and action.

Whatever circumstances so provoked Richard Glass that he was moved to call Erasmus James a "cheating rogue" and "one dyde dog" are not known. Richard's problems with Erasmus James did not end there:

> Thomas Home, aged about twenty-four years, and Sarah Comes. aged about seventeen years ;who] testified that on Sept. 13, the last day of the week at about sunset they were at Jame's house and heard Richard Glasse and John Chinn, his brother-in-law, come in a railing manner, Glasse called him names and challenged him to fight and James perceiving what a rage he was in went and shut his gate and barred it inside. Then Glass beat at it with his hands and stones, but some who were in the street persuaded him to desist. He also swore by the name of God that he would knock Jame's brains out, etc Sworn, Sept. 20, 1684, before Moses Mavencke, commissioner. (Source: Essex Institute, 1684 records.)

JOHN & JAMES GLASSES
(1690 – 1828; < Roger < James < John)
GENERATIONS 4 - 7

Roger Glass, who emigrated with his three siblings – Henry, James, and Amy – in 1637 to the Boston area, eventually settled in Duxbury,

Glass Family in America

Plymouth County, Massachusetts, just south of Boston. Roger and his descendants used the names John and James for their male descendants. This can make for considerable confusion for genealogists. However, for tracing the Glass family line that eventually appears in Nebraska in the late 1800s, it is sufficient to know that Henry's, not Roger's, great-great-grandson James was born in Connecticut in the mid-1700s.

There appear to be three John Glasses in Duxbury in the 1600s. Roger's son John, the executor of his will, was probably born about 1650. Most likely, another child named John Glass was born to Roger's son John Glass in about 1680, because it is known that a John Glass married a Martha Temple in Boston on April 1, 1703, and was living in Duxbury in 1704. John's ownership of land in Duxbury was recorded in 1714-15. In 1711, land was donated adjacent to his property for the building of the first school in Duxbury. John and Martha had two children, James, born in 1709, and Martha, born in 1704.

James Glass of Duxbury, who was born in 1709, died in 1759. He is identified as a landowner in Duxbury in 1748. He was married to Thankful Dawes. Thankful Dawes was born in September 16, 1715, at Maine, to Ambrose Dawes and Mary Dawes (born Chandler). Thankful lived many years and died on January 28, 1798.

The children of James and Thankful Glass include the following:

Esther Glass, born March 21, 1736; John Glass, born March 21, 1737-8; James Glass, born January 5, 1739; Rispah Glass, daughter born, September 11, 1742; Seriah Glass, a daughter born August 25, 1744; Ezekiel Glass, born in 1746; and a son named Consider (who went by the name Sydney), who was born one month before his father's death in 1759.

John Glass, son of James and Thankful, died January 14, 1828, in Duxbury, MA. John Glass may have had 3 sons. A John Glass is listed as a "Minute Man" of Duxbury in 1773. This could be his record of service in the Revolutionary War:

    John Glass
Service: Massachusetts   Rank: Private
Birth: 3-21-1737   Duxbury Massachusetts
Death: 1-14-1828   Duxbury Massachusetts
Service Description: 1) Capts Samuel Bradford, Ebenezer Washburn 2) Daniel Shay, Cols Cotton, Brooks

While the women of this era were occupied in the home raising the many children of the families, the men of the Plymouth Colony region were employed either as farmers or fishermen. It was a time long before the introduction of both steam engines and fertilizers, and it was necessary for a single farmer to raise enough food to support only his own family. And so ends here the account of the John and James Glasses of Duxbury, Massachusetts.

RUHAMAH AMMI WILLIS
(1670 – 1739; < Richard Willis < Amy (Glass) Willis < James Glass)
GENERATION 5

Ruhamah was born to Richard Willis and Patience Bonham in 1670 in Plymouth, Massachusetts. Ruhamah is a biblical name meaning "having obtained mercy." The name appears in the Bible as having been given to Hosea's daughter. Ruhamah died there on December 10, 1739. She married Eleazar Rogers (1673 – 1739) in Plymouth. Eleazar Rogers was a descendant of Thomas Rogers (born about 1651), a Mayflower Pilgrim and one of 41 signers of the Mayflower Compact. He was also descended from Bernard Rogers who was born in Wittenberg, Saxony, Germany in 1543. Eleazer Rogers was called a "yeoman" in 1683 and 1699, an "innholder" in 1719 and 1723, and a "seafayring Man" in 1725.

Glass Family in America

Ruhamah and Eleazar had several children.

1. Elizabeth, born October 15, 1698
2. Thomas, born October 8, 1701
3. Hannah, born February 26, 1703
4. Experience, born April 28, 1707
5. Eleazar, born October 2, 1710
6. Willis, born April 22, 1711
7. Abijah, born August 4, 1714
8. Moriah, born October 21, 1716
9. Ruth, born in 1718.

Willis, Abijah, and Ruth died in infancy; Moriah died at about age 7. The remaining children have many descendants. For example, Rumahah's son Thomas married a Priscilla Churchill in 1721 in Plymouth; they had a son named Samuel in 1728. Samuel married Hannah Bartlett on October 25, 1750, in Plymouth. Samuel and Hannah's daughter Priscilla married Thomas Linnell, and they bore eight children: Elizabeth, Israel, Uriah, Jerusha, Priscilla, Thomas Jr., Josiah, and Dean Linnell. The descendants of Amy Glasse (1618 – 1648) are extremely numerous.

JOSEPH BUMPAS
(1674 – 1739; < Wybra (Glass) Bumpas < James Glass < James Glasse)
GENERATION 5

Joseph, son of Wybra Glass and Joseph Bumpas, married Mary Ford on March 12, 1712, in Weymouth, Norfolk, Massachusetts. Joseph and Mary had nine children including a daughter: Rebecca Bumpas.

RICHARD GLASS (Jr.)
(1687 – 1741 ; < Richard Glass < Henry Glass < James Glasse)
GENERATION 5

Richard (Jr.) was born March 15, 1687, at Marblehead, Massachusetts to Richard (Sr.) and his wife, Elizabeth Fox. Richard (Jr.) spent his early years as a fisherman, his father's trade also. He lived on the shores of New Hampshire as a child. In 1712, he married Elizabeth Curteis on March 4th at Marblehead. Elizabeth was born in 1691 in Essex, Massachusetts. It is unclear exactly how many children Elizabeth bore for Richard (Jr.), but genealogists feel certain that there were three: Anthony, Stephen, and James. It is Anthony Richard Glass who is the ancestor of the MA-CT-VT-MI-NE Glass line. At about the time of the birth of these children, the family appears to have migrated from Massachusetts to the Canterbury, Connecticut area. Anthony's birthplace is commonly identified as either Manchester, Massachusetts or Canterbury, Connecticut. Elizabeth died in 1723 at age 32.

One source lists Richard's date and place of death as Pemaquid, Lincoln, Maine, on October 28, 1741. Pemaquid is an obsolete name for the town of Bristol, which is located on the rough east coast of Maine. Richard may have been a fisherman, like his father, who maintained a residence in Maine, and like his grandfather, Henry Glass.

REBECCA BUMPAS
(1713–1783; < Joseph Bumpas < Wybra (Glass) Bumpas < James Glass)
GENERATION 6

Rebecca was born on May 26, 1713, in Middleboro, Plymouth, Massachusetts. Middleboro is a village in the center of Plymouth County, adjacent to Plymouth Colony. Rebecca died on August 18, 1783, in Monson, Hampden County, Massachusetts. On June 19, 1735, Rebecca married Thomas Tupper in Middleboro. Thomas Tupper's ancestors go back to England in the 1500s and to Robert Tupper who was born in Sachsen, Germany in 1500; Robert Tupper died in England. Rebecca and Thomas had a son whom they named Joseph.

1740 Some Glass Ancestors Move to Connecticut

ANTHONY RICHARD GLASS
(About 1719 – 1800 ; < Richard Glass < Richard Glass < Henry Glass)
GENERATION 6

Anthony Richard Glass was born in 1719, probably at Manchester, Essex, Massachusetts. He married Eunice Bennett on June 19, 1740, in New London, Connecticut, and spent the rest of his life in Canterbury, Connecticut. Eunice was born on April 5, 1721, in Preston, New London, Connecticut. Anthony Glass became one of 14 founding members of the Westminster Society of Congregationalists in 1744. It is unknown where Anthony and Eunice are buried, though there is some possibility that Anthony was buried on the farm of one of his daughters, Lois, in Wells, Vermont. Ten children are known to have been born to Anthony and Eunice: Eunice (born April 28, 1742), who died at age seven on October 16, 1749; Lois (born January 1, 1743); James (born May 31, 1744); Silas (born August 30, 1746); Prudence (born March 8, 1748); Sarah (born August 20, 1751); Mary (born June 15, 1753); Rufus (born April 7, 1755); Samuel (born April 1, 1758); Eunice (born January 10, 1760). Rufus Glass fought in the Revolutionary War. It appears that Samuel also was a soldier in the Revolutionary War.

JOSEPH TUPPER
(1739–1797; < Rebecca Bumpas < Joseph Bumpas < Wybra (Glass) Bumpas)
GENERATION 7

Joseph was born on Augist 25, 1739, in Middleboro, Plymouth, Massachusetts. Joseph married Lydia Tinkham on May 1, 1779, in Middleborough. He died in Tolland, Connecticut, on July 14, 1797. Joseph Tupper's tombstone records the cause of his death as "having fallen from his horse," and that he left a wife and eleven children.

1. Daniel born on March 12, 1786
2. Jedidah, daughter, born on January 30, 1796
3. Joseph, born on January 29, 1788
4. Lovina.
5. Lydia, born on March 22, 1794
6. Mary
7. Menzo, son, born on February 8, 1792
8. Minerva, born on March 11, 1798
9. Nathaniel, born February 27, 1784. Settled in Wisconsin after the Civil War.
10. Samuel, born on January 12, 1790
11. Thomas, born on June 27, 1793

As one would expect, with all these children the Tupper line is very large. It will not be followed beyond this generation in this account of Glass descendants.

Glass Family in America

SAMUEL GLASS
(1758 – 1813 ; < Anthony Richard Glass < Richard Glass < Richard Glass)
GENERATION 7

Samuel was born on April 1, 1758, in Canterbury, Connecticut. He served in the Revolutionary War, and migrated to Vermont in about 1780, after the war. He married Abigail Munger in Wells, Rutland, Vermont. Abigail is a very distant relative of both Charlie Munger, Vice-Chairman of Berkshire-Hathaway and Jodie Foster, an actress.

Three of Samuel's six children were males: Eli, Anthony, and Calvin. Anthony died at age 13 of tuberculosis. No record of Eli's death has been found. Calvin was born on October 29, 1794, in Wells. It is Calvin's line that eventually migrated to western Illinois (Knox County, Monmouth, Galesburg) and accounts for many of that surname in that area for decades. Samuel Glass's descendants who settled in Illinois have been recorded in detail in Shaver, Robert H. (1993) *From Great Britain to Western Illinois: A Glass-Cone-Smith Genealogical Sequel to Plant a Tree by Alan E. Shaver*. Bloomington, IN.

Samuel died in Wells on April 4, 1813, in an epidemic.

1770 - 1873 Migration to Vermont, New York, and Then, Michigan

JAMES GLASS
(1744 – 1798 ; < Anthony Richard Glass < Richard Glass < Richard Glass)
GENERATION 7

James Glass was born to Anthony Richard Glass and Eunice Bennett on May 31, 1744, in Duxbury, Plymouth, Massachusetts. At some point in childhood, James and his siblings probably migrated south from Duxbury, Plymouth, Massachusetts to Canterbury, Windham, Connecticut. On October 28, 1767, James married Hannah Sufford, probably in Canterbury.

James and Hannah had two children: Parthenia, born February 23, 1769, perhaps in Canterbury, and Philetus, born in 1771. Philetus's place of birth is sometimes reported to be in Vermont. And it is highly likely that Hannah died sometime shortly after the birth of the couple's second child.

James married a second time to Ruth Bassett on August 29, 1771, in Goshen, Connecticut. Ruth bore six children: Cyrenus (born December 8, 1773 in Goshen), Heman (born 1775), Sarah (born 1777), Erastus (born 1782), and Reuben (born October 8, 1787).

A mystery: Microfilms of records of births in Whitingham, Windham County, Vermont, show the birth of Ira Glass on September 25, 1784. No other record of this Ira Glass exists, raising the possibility of early death. The same microfilm does not show the birth of Reuben in 1787.

The link between Henry Glass of Marblehead, Massachusetts, and the Glasses who eventually settled in Michigan and Nebraska hinges on the parentage of Reuben Glass who was born in Vermont in 1787. At every point where Reuben Glass reported his place of birth, he identified Vermont. His father, James, may have migrated back and forth between Connecticut and Vermont, even though in that day such movement would have been arduous and infrequent. Reuben's half-brother Philetus consistently reported his birthplace as Vermont, but Reuben's older siblings born to James and Ruth are reported to have been born in Connecticut. It is either a coincidence or a clue that Canterbury is in the Connecticut county named Windham, and James – quite probably the father of Reuben – resided for a time in Windham County, Vermont.

Unraveling the puzzle of Reuben's birth in 1787 in Vermont hinges on accounting for all of the Vermont Glass families at the end of the 18th century. The 1790 Census – the first taken in the United States – shows that there are four Glass families in Vermont.

James Glass, of Shaftsbury, Bennington County, Vermont, was a Baptist preacher. The long line of Glasses stemming from Henry, James and Roger were very likely Puritans, escaping religious persecution – and impending civil war? – by the Church of England. The James Glass of Shaftsbury was married to Rachel Warren. They had a son named Cyrus who migrated to River Falls, Wisconsin. But they were married in Amsterdam, NY in 1797, ten years after the birth of Reuben Glass.

Two other Glass families in Vermont in 1790 were the families of Rufus and Samuel Glass. Both settled in Wells, Rutland County, in 1783. It is well known that both Rufus and Samuel were the sons of James Glass of Canterbury, Connecticut, whose ancestors are found on the line that goes through Anthony Richard Glass, Richard Glass Jr. and Richard Glass Sr. back to Henry Glass, the brother of Roger Glass. But for the purpose of establishing the ancestry of Reuben Glass, it is sufficient to record that the offspring of these two men – Rufus[14] and Samuel – are

---

[14] Rufus Glass of Wells named one of his sons Rufus, and Rufus Jr. named one of his sons Reuben. This Reuben, born long after 1787, spent most of his life in

completely accounted for and could not have included Reuben Glass born in 1787.

This leaves the fourth male Glass in Vermont in 1790. A James Glass is recorded in the Census as head of household in Whitingham, Windham Co., Vermont.[15] Whitingham is approximately 150 miles northwest of Duxbury, MA, as the crow flies. It is also about 75 miles from Wells, Rutland, VT. Whitingham is also about two miles north of the New York state border in the center of Vermont. In 1784, James Glass was made a Freeman of Whitingham, Vermont. James was married twice: first to Hannah Sufford, with whom he had two children, Parthenia and Philetus, and secondly with Ruth Bassett, with whom he had several children including Reuben in 1787. In the 1790 Census, there were 12 persons in the household: 3 males under age 16, 4 males over age 16, and 5 females. Reuben would have been 3 years old in 1790. In the 1800 Census, there were 8 persons in the household: 1 male under age 10; 1 male age 10 – 15; 1 male age 16 – 25; 1 male older than 45. Reuben would have been 13 in 1800.

LeRoy, New York, and should not be confused with Reuben Glass, born in 1787, to James and Ruth Glass.

[15] Another coincidence befalling the Glass family and Mormonism (see the story of the Rufus Glass and Oliver Cowdrey families below) is that Whitingham was the birthplace of Brigham Young, in 1801.

Glass Family in America

RUFUS GLASS
(1755 – 1813; < Anthony Richard Glass < Richard Glass < Richard Glass)
GENERATION 7

Rufus was the son of James Glass (son of Anthony Richard Glass and so on back to Henry Glass) of Canterbury, Connecticut. Rufus Glass married Huldah Fuller in East Haddam, Connecticut, on November 16, 1779. Hulda Fuller was born January 26, 1762, in East Haddam, Connecticut. Hulda's Father was William Fuller; her mother was Rebecca Spencer. Hulda Fuller is the sixth generation (3rd Great Grandchild) of Edward Fuller (died 1621 in Plymouth, Massachusetts) – who came to America on the Mayflower.

Rufus served in the Revolutionary War.
    Glass, Rufus
    DAR Ancestor #: A208412
    Service: Connecticut   Rank: Private
    Birth: 4-7-1755   Canterbury Windham Co Connecticut
    Death: 4-4-1812   Wells Rutland Co Vermont
    Service Source: Johnston, Ct Men In The Rev, P 404
    Service Description: 1) Capt Holmes, Hartford Co Militia

In 1786, Rufus and Huldah moved from Connecticut to Wells, Rutland County, Vermont. They settled on a farm. At about the same time, Rufus's brother Samuel moved to Wells from Connecticut and settled on an adjoining farm. There they raised their family and eventually died in an epidemic in 1813 – Huldah on March 21st and Rufus two weeks later. As an aside, Oliver H. P. Cowdery (October 3, 1806 – March 3, 1850) was, with Joseph Smith, an important participant in the formative period of the Latter Day Saints movement between 1829 and 1836. He was the first baptized Latter Day Saint, one of the Three Witnesses of the Book of Mormon's golden plates, one of the first Latter Day Saints apostles, and the Second Elder of the church. In addition, Oliver was one of three

persons who wrote down the Book of Mormon as it was being translated by Joseph Smith. In the early 1800s, Oliver lived in the household of Rufus and Huldah Glass in Wells. Huldah and Oliver's mother, Rebecca (Fuller) Cowdrey, were sisters. Later (1820-1822) he lived in the **household** of Rufus's son **Arunah Glass**.

The number of children born to Huldah and Rufus is variously reported. Some sources say eight, others say eleven. No single source has listed the names of even ten. Most stop after naming nine offspring. The children of Rufus and Huldah include the following[16]:
Lucinda Glass, Alice Glass, William Glass (born 1787), Susannah Glass, Arunah Glass, Lucinda Glass, Roxanna Glass, Polly Glass, and Rufus Glass (Jr.).

Rufus (Jr.) would have been born in Wells, Vermont, in about 1790. It is known that a man named Rufus Glass spent most of his adult life in LeRoy, New York. In an early 19th Century U.S. Census, he is living next to a Reuben Glass, who was born in 1822 and who, in a later Census, lists his father's birthplace as Vermont. This Reuben, son of Rufus, probably had a son whom he named Reuben, who was resident in LeRoy in several Censuses and who married an Emma Brown in about 1876. It is important to note that these two Reubens are different from the Reuben Glass born to James Glass in Whitingham, Vermont who is the ancestor of the Glass descendants who migrated to Michigan and then Nebraska. These facts establish, at least, that the given name

---

[16] Source: *History of Wells, Vermont, for the First Century After Its Settlement.* Cornell University Library.

Reuben was used by the off-spring of James Glass of Canterbury, Connecticut.

GLASS, PHILETUS
(1771 – 1850 ; < James Glass < Anthony Richard Glass < Richard Glass)
GENERATION 8

Philetus Glass was born in 1771 to James Glass and Hannah Sufford. He later lived in Vermont and eventually migrated to New York State and finally to Erie, Pennsylvania, where his descendants can still be found to this day.

The Erie County, Pennsylvania Anti-Slavery Society was formed in 1836 with Colonel James M. Moorhead of Harborcreek as president and William Gray of Wayne as secretary. Other members included Philetus Glass, Dr. Smedley, and Tuttle Loomis of North East; William Himrod, A. Mehaffey and Aaron Kellog of Erie; Hamlin Russell of Millcreek; and S.C. Lee of Summit. According to documented accounts, many of these men were also involved in the Underground Railroad.

CYRENUS GLASS
(1773 – 1855 ; < James Glass < Anthony Richard < Richard Glass)
GENERATION 8

Cyrenus Glass was born in Goshen, Connecticut, to James Glass and Hannah Sufford. He appears to have migrated to Windham County, Vermont, with his father, and perhaps, other members of his family. He married Sally Lauch in Whittingham, Windham, Vermont, on December 2, 1795. He may have born a son whom he named Cyrenus who appears in the 1855 Census of Chautauqua, New York. It appears that both Philetus and Cyrenus named sons after themselves. This younger Cyrenus reports having been born in Vermont in 1793, a date that is at odds with the marriage date of his supposed father. The younger

Cyrenus married Rachel (Bradt) Glass, who was 60 in 1855; they resided in the household of Henry B. Glass, who was 37. The younger Cyrenus and his wife had a 6 year-old son named Frank. Frank married Melissa Ellis and had a son whom they named Arthur E. Glass; Arthur married Dora Hubbard in New York in 1908.

REUBEN GLASS
(1787 – 1855 ; < James Glass < Anthony Richard < Richard Glass)
GENERATION 8

Reuben[17] Glass was born to James Glass and his second wife, Ruth Bassett, in May, 1787 in Vermont. A couple of facts increase the probability that Reuben Glass is in fact the son of James Glass of Whitingham, Vermont, who in turn is a direct descendant of Henry Glass, through two Richards and Anthony Richard. Reuben Glass appears in later Censuses in New York State before migrating to Michigan. James Glass of Whitingham had sons, but their names are not known for certain, whereas the names of the sons of Rufus and Samuel Glass are well established and do not include Reuben. In fact, Rufus Glass of Wells, Vermont, had a son named William in 1787, the same year in which Reuben Glass was probably born to James Glass of Whitingham. Furthermore, Reuben named one of his sons James (born in 1821, died in 1848).

The descendants of Roger Glass are numerous in the area of Duxbury, Plymouth, Massachusetts in the mid-1700s and early 1800s. The name Reuben Glass appears twice: once as the child of Nathaniel and Sarah Glass (born January 13, 1813), and of Sirajah (or Zorajah, as it was sometimes recorded) and Hannah Glass (died on June 10, 1813). All this does is establish the use of the given name Reuben among the

---

[17] The name "Reuben" is biblical, appearing in the Torah as the eldest son of Jacob and Leah and meaning "Behold, a son."

descendants of Roger Glass. Moreover, a later descendant of Roger's was named Edwin Glass, a name common to the descendants of Reuben Glass of the VT-NY-MI-NE migration. It seems quite likely that the Reuben Glass, who is the main subject from Generation 8 of this genealogy, is descended from Henry Glass, and not either of his brothers James or Roger; but it may never be known for certain that this is the case.

Sources that list Reuben Glass's father as Philetus Glass – a well known resident of Erie, PA, and member of a noted abolitionist family who served as a key nexus on the Underground Railroad – are almost certainly in error. Philetus Glass (Sr.) was born about 16 years before Reuben, and is a half-brother to Reuben. Philetus's mother was Hannah Sufford whereas Reuben's mother was Ruth Bassett.

The Census and several other sources indicate that Reuben was born in 1787, probably in May, and almost certainly in Vermont and highly likely in Whittingham, Windham County. Reuben Glass may have married Anna Wells in 1808 at the Reformed Protestant Dutch Church of Amsterdam, New York. Amsterdam, New York is less than 100 miles west of Whitingham, Vermont.[18] Anna was born on October 27, 1790. By 1812, Reuben and Anna had migrated first to Westford, Otsego, New York (about 30 miles west of Amsterdam) then to Bath, New York, which is about 150 miles further west.

Reuben and Anna's children are as follows:

1. Zenas W. Glass born 1812, Westford, Otsego, NY.
2. Harriet Glass born 1814
3. Hannah Ann Glass born December 1815
4. Almira Glass born January 1819

---

[18] The presence of Reuben Glass in Amsterdam, New York, reinforces the possibility that his father's name was James Glass, since the death of a James Glass in Amsterdam in 1798 is reported in some genealogies.

5. James Glass born November 10, 1821; he died in Michigan on April 20, 1848.
6. Isaac James Glass born September 12, 1823 in Bath, New York; he died April 12, 1909 in Livonia, Michigan.
7. Edgar M. Glass born about 1825 in Bath, New York; he died at age 14 in Michigan.
8. Emory P. Glass born August 1, 1828 in Bath, New York. He died on September 20, 1901 in Livonia, Michigan.
9. Sarah Melissa Glass born November 28, 1830, in Bath, NY
10. Roswell, dates of birth and death both unknown.[19]

Reuben Glass appears in the 1830 Census of Bath Township, Steuben County, New York, as head of household containing 2 males ages 0-5, 2 males ages 5-10, one male age 15-20 (Zenas W.), and one male age 30-40, himself. Females in the household were 2 between the ages of 5 and 10, 1 between ages 10 and 15, and one between the ages of 20 and 25.

Reuben migrated to the village of Nankin, Livonia Township, Michigan, from New York State in 1832. His wife Anna died on April 20, 1840, in Michigan. Reuben remarried a Lucy Fraser, a descendant of Dutch immigrants who very early migrated to America. They were married on January 25, 1841 in Oakland, Michigan.

An agricultural census in Wayne County, Michigan, gives a rough picture of Reuben's success as a farmer. He owned 80 acres, 60 of which were listed as "Improved." The cash value of his land was $2,000, which in 2016 money might be between $50,000 and $60,000. His farm

---

[19] The name "Roswell" appears in a list of Reuben's children that is handwritten on a page that has been inserted into Reuben's will. No other evidence that Reuben had a son named Roswell can be found. "Roswell Glass" can be found in Michigan around 1900 as a descendant of Franklin Glass, who was born in England in the early 1800s. The note inserted in the papers accompanying Reuben's will may have been the result of a fishing expedition looking for descendants.

Glass Family in America

had 3 horses, 3 milk cows, 4 cattle, 22 sheep, 5 pigs, whose total value was estimated at $359. In 1850, he produced 150 bushels of "Indian corn" and 200 bushels of oats.

Reuben died in Michigan on October 8, 1855. He is buried in the Newburgh Cemetery near Livonia, Michigan. Anna, Reuben's wife, died on April 20, 1840, in Nankin and is buried in the Newburgh Cemetery.

With Reuben's son Zenas, all doubt about parentage and other facts concerning Glass descendants disappears.

Reuben's arrival in the 1830s and his daughter-in-law's departure from Nankin some 70 years later mark nearly three-quarters of a century of the Glass family's residence in this tiny village.

Although the name is no longer officially used, the area once known as Nankin is roughly 15 miles directly west of downtown Detroit. The towns of Westland and Livonia now occupy that space.

From Wikipedia:
> Three Algonquin tribes - Potawatomi, Ojibwa, and Ottawa - met each year on the middle fork of the Rouge

Glass Family in America

River at the site of Nankin Mills to establish hunting territories. In 1829, it was proposed that Bucklin Township be divided into Lima and Richland. Due to name conflicts under territorial law prohibiting duplication of post office names, the bill was amended; Lima was renamed Nankin Township, after the Chinese city Nanking, and Richland was renamed Pekin Township, after Peking. In 1833, Pekin was renamed Redford Township, and its southern portion was subsequently set off as Dearborn Township. In 1834, Plymouth Township's southern portion became Canton Township, named after Canton, Imperial China. In 1835, Livonia Township (now the city of Livonia) was split off from Nankin. There was a post office called East Nankin beginning in 1857. Garden City, Inkster, and Wayne then incorporated from land either partially or wholly within Nankin Township. The remainder of the township incorporated as the city of Westland, effective May 16, 1966. The city took its name from a mall and was the fourth largest city in Wayne County when it incorporated.

Descriptions of 18th century life in Nankin give some insight into the conditions under which these ancestors must have lived nearly two hundred years ago. This description is taken from http://www.nankinmills.org/history.htm:

> The first Europeans came to the township to settle the land in the early 1820's. It was not an easy life they found. There were few roads through what was then wilderness. In 1825, a trip between Detroit and Ann Arbor would take more than two days. One early author described the area as "a dense unbroken wilderness teeming with wolves, bears and deer." Dysentery and malaria were constant threats and few medical services were available. But it was good land and the area began to grow and prosper.

ZENAS W. GLASS
(1812 – 1857 ; < Reuben Glass < James Glass < Anthony Richard Glass)
GENERATION 9

Zenas[20] (misspelled Genas in the 1850 U.S. Census) would have migrated to Wayne County, Michigan, some time after 1830. He settled in the Village of Nankin, some 15 miles from the center of present-day Detroit, in the area now known as Livonia, Michigan.

Zenas appears in a special 1850 agricultural census of Wayne county living on a farm adjacent to the farm of his father Reuben. The cash value of his 80 acres (40 acres "Improved") is listed as $2000, equal to about $50,000 to $60,000 in 2016 money. His livestock consisted of 4 horses, 4 milk cows, 2 cattle, 20 sheep, and 13 oxen. His livestock was valued at $322.

On January 13, 1839, he married Sarah Jane Ferris in Nankin. Sarah was born on August 22, 1821, and died in Lincoln, Nebraska, on February 24, 1923, having lived nearly 102 years. She is buried in Wyuka Cemetery in Lincoln.

---

[20] The name Zenas appears earlier in the Glass line. Zenas Thomas Glass was born to Ezekiel Glass (son of John Glass and Bernice Delano) on September 9, 1775, in Plymouth, Massachusetts. Zenas died in 1891 in Plymouth. The 1860 Census lists his occupation as Fish Peddler, owning real estate valued at $1,400. This coincidence of names reinforces the possibility that Reuben Glass descends from the Anthony Richard Glass family of Plymouth County, Massachusetts, even though Reuben was born in Vermont.

Glass Family in America

Sarah Jane (Ferris, Perrin, Stephenson) Glass wrote a letter on April 27, 1910, at the urging of her children recounting some of her life experiences.

> A little of my life's experiences, at the urgent request of my children.
>
> I was born August 22nd, 1821, in Elizabethtown, Essex County, State of New York. My mother died soon after I was 4 years old. I lived at home until 8 years of age then with a cousin on my father's side for nearly 2 years. Then with an uncle on my mother's side until 13 years old.
>
> In the meantime, I learned to spin wool and flax. I seemed to be the only one who could be spared from home, but spinning was learned at home. Was not brought up in idleness in either place.
>
> In 1836, I left my dear father's home with a married sister for a home in Michigan. Arrived in Detroit the fourth of July after a three weeks journey by canal and Lake Erie. We were both sick with ague and fever a great deal of the time.
>
> I worked at housework and nursing, when not sick. At 15, was baptized and a young man and his sister, who were strangers to me, joined at the same time. Have been a member of the M.E. church ever since. Have made many mistakes, not meaningly. ["M.E." stands for Methodist Episcopal Church, a term used to designate the Methodist Church in the northern U.S. The "Episcopal" refers to a form a governance and not the Anglican Church.]
>
> In 1839, was married to your father [Zenas W. Glass] on January 13th, being past 17 years old and your father was 25.

Glass Family in America

We lived together over 18 years, he dying and leaving me with a family of six children. Will not attempt to describe the difficulties that were passed through, which were many as there were only 2 of the children old enough to help provide for our family. I sewed, worked, house cleaned and nursed to help provide. God helped me, gave me good health. Milton, my eldest, enlisted in the war of the Rebellion in 1864 [date is in error]. That was another trial. Seemed I could not spare him. While he was in the war, I married again [Isaac F. Perrin]. Lived within a 4 mile radius of the vicinity where I first landed, with the exception of 2 years, for a period of 65 years. [Milton enlisted in the 16th Regiment of the Michigan Volunteer Infantry on August 15th, 1861 and died from wounds sustained some time after the Battle of Cold Harbor in Baltimore in the summer of 1864.]

If I could have written my life's experience as they came, it might have been easier, but to bring it up and live it over, I cannot. It breaks me all up. When this life is over, I hope to be where there is no more sin or sorrow. My great desire is to see my children that are left to me, Christians, trying to make a better world. That would rejoyce my heart more than anything else.   [Signed] Sarah Jane Stephenson

Sarah Jane Ferris and Zenas W. Glass had the following children:

1. Ellen Glass was born about 1840. She died in Michigan on November 16, 1893.
2. Cornelia Glass was born in 1842.

3. Milton C. Glass was born in 1840. He died the summer of 1864 in Baltimore after having been injured some time after the Battle of Cold Harbor in Hanover Co., VA.
4. Martha Ann Glass was born on February 6, 1842, in Michigan. She died on March 27, 1845, in Michigan.
5. Reuben E. Glass was born on November 13, 1846, in Wayne Co., Michigan. He died on October 11, 1905, in Custer County, Nebraska. He married Margaret Louise Mitchell. He married Lina Ferguson about 1865 in Wayne County, Michigan. She died before 1873. When Reuben was 18 years-old, he enlisted in the Union Army on September 5, 1864, at Redford, Michigan, as a Private. On September 6, 1864, he mustered into "D" Co. MI 24th Infantry. He was listed as "Joined Regiment on September 18, 1864, Weldon Railroad, Virginia." He was mustered out on June 30, 1865, at Detroit, Michigan.
6. Martha Glass was born about 1847.
7. Sarah Glass was born on October 7, 1848. She and her husband, Origen Frost, were the first of the Glass family to migrate to Nebraska. Two brothers, Reuben and Edwin, followed.
8. Ellen E. Glass was born in 1852 in Michigan. She probably died young.
9. Edwin Zenis Glass was born on April 4, 1857, in Nankin, Michigan. He died on January 5, 1933, in Lincoln, Nebraska. He married Eveline ("Eva") Gillett, daughter of Ira Gillett and Catherine Atherton March 23, 1881, in Perrinsville, Michigan. Eva was born on July 11, 1858, in Wayne County, Michigan. She died on July 28, 1923, in Lincoln, Nebraska.

ISAAC JAMES GLASS
(1823 – 1909; < Reuben Glass < James Glass < Anthony Richard Glass)
GENERATION 9

Isaac James Glass was born in New York State in 1823. He appears in the 1850 U.S. Census as a resident of Livonia, Michigan, married to

Eliza Ann (Finley) Glass, age 21, with three children: Mary Ann, age 5; Harriet F., age 2; Emily, age 3 months. His occupation is listed as "Farmer." The 1860 Census shows the arrival of two new children: Emma L., age 10, and Frank, age 2.

The 1870 Census reports Isaac as living in the town of Lincoln, Washington County, Kansas. None of his family appears in the same domicile. Perhaps he traveled to Kansas to homestead. By 1880, Isaac is back in Michigan, living in Genoa, Livingston County (about 25 miles northwest of Livonia), married to 35 year-old Clarisa E. Glass, and with a stepchild in the household, Nellie Barnes, age 8. (One source lists Nellie Barnes as the child of Clarisa Barnes and Oscar White. The date and place of birth are consistent with other information, but no supporting documentation exists at this time.)

So it appears that the Isaac-Eliza marriage was broken sometime between 1860 and 1870. Isaac went off to Kansas, but soon returned to Michigan and made a new family with Clarisa, whose married name might have been Barnes.

Isaac died on April 12, 1909, in Livonia and is buried in Howell, Livingston County, Michigan, which is 20 miles northwest of Livonia, Michigan.

EMORY P. GLASS
(1828 – 1901; Reuben Glass < James Glass < Anthony Richard Glass)
GENERATION 9

Emory Glass was born in Bath, New York, to Reuben and Anna on August 1, 1828. He married Lucy Almina Van Duyn (1834 – 1912) in 1865 in Livonia, Michigan. Lucy was a descendant of Cornelis Gerretse Van Duyn who was born in the Netherlands in about 1600. Emory and Lucy had

six children, three of whom, all girls, died in infancy: Hattie A., the possible twins, Loretta A., and Lorena I. A fourth daughter, Anna L. Glass was born in 1868, but nothing more is known of her. The two known surviving children are James Eddy Glass, born on September 8, 1866, and Jennie M. Glass, born in 1870.

Emory died on September 20, 1901, in Livonia, and is buried there. There are likely many descendants with the surname Glass living in the area west of Detroit. For example, James married Mary Sarah Bredin and had five children: Howard Bredin Glass (1893 – 1978); Camilla I. (1894 – 1956); Ethel L. (1895 – 1913); Emory James Glass (1898 – 1971); and Ivan W. Glass (1907 – 1913)

SARAH MELISSA (GLASS) OSBAND
(1830 – 1905; Reuben Glass < James Glass < Anthony Richard Glass)
GENERATION 9

Sarah was born on 28 November 28, 1830, in Bath, Steuben, New York. She married William Henry Osband, who was born on December 12, 1820, in Palmyra, New York. They had two sons: Norman H. Osband and Edgar Osband. Edgar was born in 1850. Sarah and William also had a daughter whom they named Rosetta M. Osband. Descendants of the two sons are not known. Norman may have died young; he is buried in Newburg Cemetery in Livonia, Michigan. The 1880 U.S. Census shows Edgar E. Osband resident in Nankin, Wayne County, Michigan. He is 48 years old and is married to Sarah E. Osband. They have two children: William W. Osband, age 19, and Meda Lo, age 13.

The Osband family came from Rhode Island, where they can be found in the early 1700s. Sarah died on August 29, 1905, in Flint, Michigan. Sarah is probably buried in Newburgh Cemetery, Livonia, Michigan.

Glass Family in America

MILTON C. GLASS
(1840 – 1865; < Zenas Glass < Reuben Glass < James Glass)
GENERATION 10

Milton C. Glass was the son of Zenas W. Glass, grandson of Reuben Glass. Milton's middle name might have been Collins or even Calvin. His nephew, Edwin Origen Glass, used Collins as the middle name of one child and Calvin as the middle name of another.

The following account of Milton Glass's service in the Civil War has been compiled from several different sources on the internet. Citing the sources individually would merely interrupt the narrative and serve little purpose when it is possible to find multiple overlapping sources by searching on entire long phrases or sentences. However, the bulk of the material can be found at
http://www.migenweb.org/michiganinthewar/infantry/16thinf.htm

> Milton enlisted in the 16th Regiment of the Michigan Volunteer Infantry on August 15th, 1861. The Sixteenth was organized at Detroit and was originally known as "Stockton's Independent Regiment" as it was organized by Colonel Thomas B. W. Stockton, Flint. It was mustered into service September 8, 1861, with an enrollment of 761 officers and men. The Regiment left Detroit for Washington, D.C., on September 16, 1861, to join the Army of the Potomac. It went into camp at Hall's Hill, Va. for the winter of 1861-62. The Sixteenth took part in the Peninsular Campaign under General McClellan and formed a part of the Third Brigade, First Division, Fifth Corp then commanded by Fitz John Porter, and remained a part of that Corp during its entire term of services.

The Regiment was at the Seige of Yorktown in April, 1862, and participated in the engagement at Hanover Court House, Virginia in May of 1862. On June 27th, it fought in one of the most desperate battles of the war at Gaines Mills, Virginia, where it gallantly contested with the Confederates for the possession of the field.

The Regiment, under command of Lieutenant Colonel Welch, was engaged at Malvern Hill, July 1; then on August 30, they participated in the battle of Manassas, where it was exposed to a destructive fire and gallantly fought heavy masses of Confederates with no thought of yielding the field.

The Regiment was at Harpers Ferry, November 1, and marched to the Rappahannock River, crossing at Falmouth and participated in the battle of Fredricksburg, where it met with heavy losses. After a series of marches, it was engaged at Chancellorsville and took an important part in that disastrous battle, but held the ground it was assigned to hold though repeatedly charged by the Southern forces.

At Middleburg, Virginia, June 21st, the Regiment fought a series of spirited engagements following and driving the Confederates for thirteen miles and went into camp at the close of the day's operations near Upperville. Colonel Stockton resigned May 8, 1863, and Lieutenant Colonel Welch was commissioned Colonel May 18, 1863. Under his command the Regiment entered upon the Pennsylvania Campaign and fought in the historic battle of Gettysburg adding a worldwide fame to its laurels in the defence of Little Round Top.

After the battle of Gettysburg, the Sixteenth crossed the mountains and started the pursuit of the Confederate army over the Potomac River at Berlin on the 17th. It was constantly on the march, skirmishing and fighting and participating in the different movements with the army of the Potomac. The months of August, September, October and during the year marched over 800 miles.

In these two years, 1862 – 1863, Milton had participated in many of the bloodiest battles of the Civil War. In December, 1863, Milton was among the 294 members of the Sixteenth who re-enlisted, and the Regiment returned to Michigan on veteran furlough. It was during the furlough of the regiment in 1863 that Milton returned to Nankin and his family for the holidays. He received a diary as a gift, perhaps, which he began keeping in early 1964. This diary is now, in the year 2016, in the possession of Jason Glass. It recounts the events of the first half of 1864, and ends at the beginning of the Battle of Cold Harbor. On August 15, 1864, Milton took part in the Siege of Petersburg. Milton was wounded at some point after that, and was transported to a military hospital in Baltimore where he died on March 1, 1865. His rank was 1st Sergeant. He is buried in the Newburgh Cemetery in Livonia, Michigan.

1873 WESTWARD MOVEMENT TO NEBRASKA

REUBEN E. GLASS
(1846 – 1905; < Zenas Glass < Reuben Glass < James Glass)
GENERATION 10

Reuben E. Glass was born on November 13, 1846, in Nankin, Wayne County, Michigan. He married Margaret Louise Mitchell. He married Lina Ferguson about 1865 in Wayne County, MI. She died before 1873. At age 18, he enlisted in the Union army at Redford, Michigan, as a Private. He joined his regiment on September 18, 1864, at Weldon Railroad, VA. He was mustered out on June 30, 1865, at Detroit.

Plattsmouth, NE 1874

Glass Family in America

The following biographical information is based on his entry in *Custer County Biographies:*

In the death of Reuben E. Glass, who spent the last years of his life retired from active life, in Broken Bow, Nebraska, Custer County, lost one of its most valuable citizens. He had been a resident of the state since 1873 and during that time he had become well known and had made many friends who appreciated his character and worth. Mr. Glass was born in Detroit, Michigan, November 13, 1846, third of the six children born to Zenas and Sarah (Ferris) Glass, natives of New York. The father died in Michigan, and the mother survives, making her home in Lincoln, Nebraska. Of their children: one son, Milton, died in the Civil war; one son, Edwin Z., lives in Lincoln; one daughter, Mrs. Sarah Frost, lives in Lincoln; others are deceased.

Mr. Glass grew to manhood's estate on a Michigan farm, receiving his education in local schools. He served in the civil war as a member of Company D, Twenty-fourth Michigan Infantry, where he won a creditable record, and after leaving the service returned to Michigan, where he engaged in business in the line of retail drugs. His first wife was Mrs. Lina Ferguson, who died in Michigan, leaving one daughter, Mrs. Lizzie Nichols, who has since died.

In 1873, Mr. Glass came to Plattsmouth, Cass County, Nebraska, where he engaged in the drug business, and there, on February 3, 1876, he married Miss Margaret Louise

Mitchell, who was born in Iowa and came to Cass County in 1874.

In 1878, Mr. and Mrs. Glass moved to Kearney, Nebraska, where they spent two years, but on account of failing health he was obliged to give up his business, and in March, 1880, they came to Custer County and he took a homestead of one hundred and sixty acres on the South Loup river where they remained ten years. He also pre-empted one hundred and sixty acres of land, and in 1897 or 1898 purchased one hundred and sixty acres of land on section nineteen, township seventeen range twenty, although he never lived on the latter place, which Mrs. Glass now owns. In December, 1891, Mr. Glass retired from farm life and purchased a comfortable residence in Broken Bow, which continued as his home until his death, October 11, 1905. He was survived by his widow, who still lives in the home, where she has every comfort and is surrounded by a large circle of sincere friends. Mr. Glass was a staunch Presbyterian in religious views and stood ready to help any religious or beneficial movement in his County or state. He died in the prime of life, and his death came as a shock to his many friends and acquaintances, among whom his loss was deeply deplored. He was regarded as a public-spirited citizen and highly esteemed by all. [End of entry in *Custer County Biographies*]

SARAH (GLASS) FROST
(1848 – 1939; < Zenas Glass < Reuben Glass < James Glass)
GENERATION 10

Sarah Glass was born on October 7, 1848, in Nankin Township, Michigan. She died on November 17, 1939, in Council Bluffs, Iowa. She married Origen Frost in Michigan in about 1870.

Sarah and her husband moved to Nebraska to the town of Plattsmouth in 1872. Origen also appears as a resident of Lincoln, Nebraska, in 1873, employed as a conductor on the Burlington & Missouri Railroad. His residence was on 7th Street between P & Q Streets. This area is where the train depot was located, so he may have been a roomer there in connection with his work on the railroad. Sharah was soon followed to Nebraska by two of her brothers: Reuben E. and Edwin Z.

Sarah and Origen had at least two sons: Milton David Frost, born in December, 1872, probably in Nebraska; Reuben Origen Frost, born in 1887 in Nebraska.

EDWIN ZENIS GLASS
(1857 – 1933 ; < Zenas < Reuben < James)
GENERATION 10

Edwin Zenis Glass is of special interest in this genealogy because he is the first male member (thus making possible the tracing of the surname) of the Glass family to relocate from Michigan to Nebraska. As was already pointed out, Edwin Zenis was born in Nankin Township, Michigan, on April 4, 1857. Edwin was too young to have served in the Union army in the Civil War, unlike his brothers Milton and Reuben.

Edwin appears in the 1870 Census as residing in the household of James H. Stephenson (misspelled Stevenson) along with his mother and his sister Ellen. He is 13 years-old at the time. According to family lore, Edwin and his stepfather did not get along, and Edwin left the household shortly after the 1870 Census. Neither he nor Ellen appears in the Stephenson household in subsequent Censuses. In 1873, at the age of 16, Edwin traveled west – probably in the company of his brother Reuben E. – and for a short time took up residence at the home of his sister and brother-in-law, Sarah and Origen Frost[21] in Plattsmouth, Nebraska. A state census taken in 1876 shows four persons in the Origen Frost

---

[21] Origen Frost was born in Michigan in about 1841. The Frost family goes back as far as 1660, where they were located in the state of Maine. He married Sarah Glass in Michigan in 1874. They had at least two children: Milton and Reuben. Origen died on December 1, 1909.

Glass Family in America

household: Milton D. Frost, age 3; Edwin Glass, age 18; Sarah A. Frost, age 27; and Origen Frost, age 35.

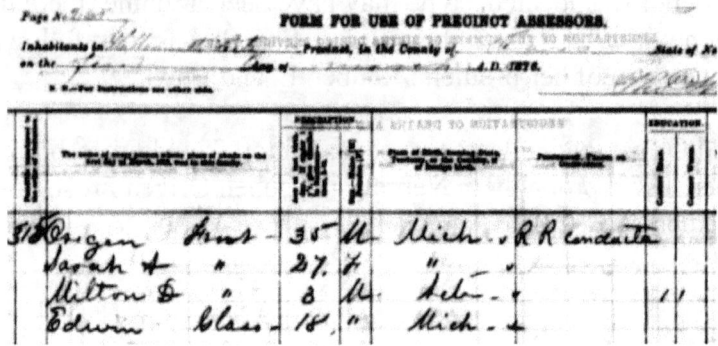

The 1880 Federal Census lists Origen's occupation as Railroad Conductor and his residence as Omaha. That same Census finds Edwin in a boarding house in Plattsmouth. As a resident of Plattsmouth, Origen Frost would have been employed as a conductor on the Burlington railroad. The Burlington completed its connection to Lincoln, Nebraska, in 1870. Edwin secured employment with the railroad and served as an engineer throughout his adult life. It is likely that he took up residence in Lincoln in connection with his employment by the CB&Q in about 1878.

Edwin returned to Michigan briefly to marry Eveline ("Eva") Gillett on March 23, 1881, who thereafter followed him back to Nebraska. (See BRIEF BIOGRAPHIES.) By 1880, the couple had settled in Lincoln, Nebraska, where their only child, Edwin Origen Glass was born on November 25, 1883.

The 1910 Census shows that Edwin's mother, Sarah Ferris, and sister, Sarah Frost, lived with him and Eva in Lincoln. Edwin Z. Glass appears in the 1915 Lincoln City

Directory, residing at 3410 J Street; he was employed as an engineer on the Burlington & Maryland Railway.

Edwin Zenis Glass died in Lincoln on January 5, 1933, at age 75. He is buried there in Wyuka Cemetery.

MILTON DAVID FROST
(1872 – 1957; < Sarah < Zenas < Reuben)
GENERATION 11

Milton was born on December 25, 1872. He was likely born in Nebraska. He died on August 26, 1957, in Oakland, Almeda, California. Milton was a machinist on the CB&Q railroad. He lived for many years in Blue Springs, Nebraska, which is about 40 miles south of Lincoln on Highway 77.

Milton was married on May 24, 1899, to Belle Naomi Taylor, who was born on January 8, 1875, in Schoffners Corners, Jefferson, Pennsylvania, and died on January 5, 1939, in Alameda, California. They had two sons: Kenneth Lyle Frost (born in 1910 in Nebraska) and Claude T. Frost (born in 1902 in Wyoming).

Milton Frost, left, with a cousin. 1900. Adams, NE

REUBEN ORIGEN FROST
(1887 – 1978; Sarah < Zenas < Reuben)
GENERATION 11

Reuben was born in Stromsburg, Nebraska, in 1887, while his father was employed by the railroad. In 1910, Reuben resided in Council Bluffs, Iowa. Frost was a chief clerk with the Railway Postal Service. He retired in 1952 after 47 years of service. He was also a member of the St. Peter's Church, Knights of Columbus, Drumm General Assembly and Chalice Club of the fourth degree Knights of Columbus, the

Glass Family in America

National Association of Retired Employees and the Railway Postal Transportation Association.

He married Margarite Marie Shea (1889 – 1966) in Council Bluffs on June 23, 1911. He appears in the 1930 federal Census living in Council Bluffs, Pottawattamie, Iowa, when he was 43 years old. His wife Margarite was born in Iowa. Margarite's father was born in Cork, Ireland.

The following children were in the household:

1. Bernice M. (1913 - ?)

2. Eileen Dorthy   (1915 1969)

3. Roderick Joseph (1923 – 1999)

4. Marilyn (1931 - ?)

5. Jacquelyn Ann (1931 - ?)

Marilyn and Jacqueline Ann may have been twins.

Reuben died on July 28, 1978. Marguerite's obituary reveals something about the later lives and locations of her and Reuben's children:

> MARGUERITE M. FROST, 77, died Wednesday at a local hospital after a long illness. A lifelong resident of Council Bluffs, she was a member of St. Patrick's Catholic Church and its Catholic Daughters of America. Mrs. Frost and her husband, Reuben O., celebrated their 55th wedding anniversary last June. Other survivors include: Mrs. Bernice Colton of Council Bluffs, Mrs. Eileen Smith of Redondo Beach, California, Mrs. Marilyn Stephens of North Platte, Nebraska, and Miss Jacquelyn Frost of Phoenix, Arizona; son, Roderick J. of Council

Bluffs; 14 grandchildren and eight great-grandchildren.

Seated left to right: Sarah Jane (Ferris) Glass, Reuben O. Frost (grandson of Sarah Jane), possibly Eileen Frost. Standing left to right: Possibly Bernice Frost, Sarah (Glass) Frost (daughter of Sarah Jane). Photo taken in about 1920 in Lincoln, Nebraska, shortly before Sarah Jane's death in 1923 at age 102.

Glass Family in America

EDWIN ORIGEN GLASS
(1883 – 1960 ; < Edwin Zenis < Zenas < Reuben)
GENERATION 11

Edwin Origen Glass was born in Lincoln, Nebraska, on November 25, 1883, to his parents Edwin Zenis Glass and Eveline (Gillett) Glass. His middle name was taken from that of Edwin Zenis's brother-in-law, Origen Frost.

In 1906, Edwin Z. Glass purchased 320 acres in Perkins County in western Nebraska. The property is located about 6 miles north and 3 miles east of Grant, Nebraska (Section 9, T.11N. R.38 W. at the intersection of County Roads 766 & 331) and constitutes the west half of the section. He sent his son Edwin Origen Glass to Grant to farm the property. The map below shows the grant of land to the Union Pacific Railroad in return from the construction of the rail line. All land 20 miles each side of the railway was given to the company by an act of Congress in 1850. The land purchased by Edwin Z. Glass is 10 miles south of Ogallala.[22]

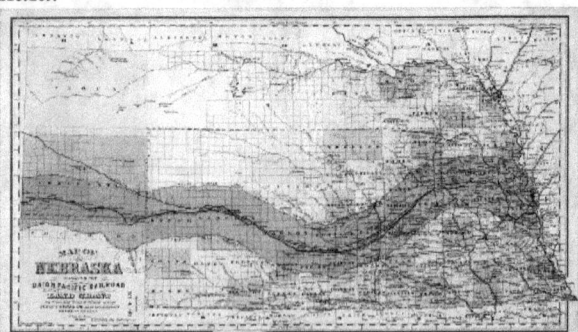

---

[22] Perkins County was not incorporated until 1887, and so it does not appear on the map.

An abstract of title to the land shows the 320 half-section having passed through several owners between 1887 and 1918. The federal government granted the land to the Union Pacific Railway Company on April 25, 1887. (The transcontinental railway was completed at Promontory Point in Utah in 1869.) Union Pacific sold the land to E. H. Seaman on March 22, 1894 for $640 (equal to approximately $17,000 in 2016 buying power). Seaman sold the property to W. L. Rutledge on October 6, 1902, for $1 who immediately sold the property to Fred E. Eppler for $1; Eppler mortgaged the property for $400.

On September 15, 1906, the property was purchased by Edwin Z. Glass and his wife Eva for the sum of $1,500. By 1918, when Edwin Zenis sold the property to C. W. Watkins, Edwin had acquired the entire section. (A section is one square mile and contains 640 acres.) The purchase price paid by Watkins was $18,000 – equal in 2016 buying power to $285,000.

It was in Perkins County that Edwin O. Glass met and married Nora Ellen Jones on November 25, 1908. Ellen had been born on September 20, 1888 at Imperial, Nebraska, which is 28 miles southeast of Grant, Nebraska. Ellen was the daughter of Wilson Ballard Avery Jones and Emma Boardman Bragg. It's unclear when the family came to western Nebraska, but it was probably in the early 1880s. Jones was of Welsh descent with known ancestors in Wales in the mid-1500s. Family lore maintains that he was alcoholic and abandoned the family at some point much later after migrating to Nebraska.[23] Ellen maintained a life-long aversion to alcohol. Wilson Ballard Avery Jones died on Christmas Eve, 1926 in Medway, Hamilton County, Kansas, and was buried in Syracuse, Kansas. Through Wilson's mother, Elizabeth Ann Miller and her father, Brice Miller, the line can be traced back to James Wolfe, the hero of the Battle of the Plains of Abraham[24]. The Bragg line is also quite well known and likewise can be traced to Virginia and to the early settlement of the colony.

Ellen recalled being fearful as a child due to the recent wars between the Sioux tribe and the U.S. military in western Nebraska, that did not end until 1890.

Edwin and Ellen's first child, Edwin Orville, was born at Grant on August 24, 1909. The name Orville seems not to have appeared in the Glass line before this generation. It is more than idle speculation to suggest that the popular use of the name Orville may have originated with the Wright brothers, whose first successful flight of a heavier than air plane took place in December of 1903. In fact, the use of the name Orville as a boy's name reached a peak in 1910 at a rate of about 12 per 10,000; Wilbur was used at the rate of 18 per 10,000 in the same time frame. Two more sons were born at Grant: Milton Collins Glass on May 30, 1911, and Lyle Calvin Glass on November 20, 1913.

---

[23] There is likely some truth to this family fable. By 1910, Wilson no longer appears in the same household as Emma. The 1920 US Census shows "Ballard Jones," age 66 living as a boarder in West Virginia; his occupation is listed as "peddler." His marital status is listed as "Divorced." Emma Jones appears in the 1925 Kansas Census living with her son Samuel in Kansas. Wilson returns to Samuel's home at some point after 1920 and dies there in 1926.

[24] Major General James Wolfe was a British officer, known for his training reforms but remembered chiefly for his victory over the French battle at the Battle of the Plains of Abraham in Canada in 1759. The battle secured Canada for the British.

Dry land farming was not successful in western Nebraska in the early1900s. The farm may have prospered for a brief while. Between 1910 and 1915, Edwin built a home for the family at the

farm. The house was still in use in 2010, but was moved to Hershey, Nebraska, and renovated by the new owner. Two consecutive years, 1915 & 1916, of hail left the family in dire circumstances. In 1917, the family left Grant and returned to Lincoln, living for a short time in the southeast neighborhood known as College View. They had sold their farm for $18,000 to C. A. Watkins. Edwin Zenis made out quite nicely on the sale of the land; it's unclear to what extent his son, Edwin Origen, benefitted from the transaction.

The family – parents, Orville, Milton, and Lyle – lived in Lincoln for one year before moving to Syracuse, Kansas. Edwin and Ellen found a deserted sod house in Sharon Springs, Kansas, about 30 miles directly north of Syracuse. They lived there for a year or two, and their fourth son, Victor Buren Glass, was born there on September 20, 1918. Orville and Milton attended school in **Sharon Springs, Kansas**.

Glass Family in America

After another brief sojourn in Lincoln, the family moved to Olney Springs, Colorado, in 1920. Olney Springs lies 40 miles west of Pueblo, Colorado, in the Arkansas River Valley. Their fifth and last son, Warren Gayland Glass, was born at Olney Springs on February 20, 1920.

The family's fortunes fared no better in Olney Springs than they had in Sharon Springs or in Grant. In the afternoon of June 3, 1921, a cloudburst opened up over Pueblo, Colorado. The Denver Weather Bureau reported more than six inches fell from the skies that week in 1921, drenching Pueblo from June 3 to June 5. The rain was fearsome; the damage after the floodwater receded was worse. More than 600 homes were carried away, according to historic records, causing what would equate to more than $300 million in damage by today's standards. The Arkansas River had reached higher than 15 feet in some areas. The entire Arkansas Valley, from 30 miles west of Pueblo to the Colorado–Kansas state line, was severely flooded. Hundreds of people died, with some death toll estimates as high as 1,500. Irrigation channels were destroyed throughout the entire Arkansas River Valley, including those that supported the farm of Edwin and Ellen Glass and their sons.

In mid-1921, Edwin and Orville struck out for greener pastures in Edwin's homeland, Lincoln, Nebraska. Orville recalls a trip by train for part of the way and having hocked an Ingersoll watch in eastern Kansas to make the final leg of the trip to Lincoln. Having arranged for lodging in Lincoln – Edwin Origen's father still lived in Lincoln until his death in 1933 – they probably sent for the remainder of the family. Whether Ellen negotiated the journey without adult assistance with her remaining four sons is not known.

The family may have lived for a short time with or near Edwin's father, Edwin Zenis, in an area of southeast Lincoln known as College View. On June 10, 1926, the only daughter of Edwin and Ellen was born: Eva Ann. "Eve-Ann," as she was called, died at the age on 10 on June 28, 1936, possibly as the result of complications from an appendectomy.

Milton, Lyle and Orville

At some point in the mid-1920s, the family took up residence at 4104 G Streets in Lincoln. That home remained the residence of Edwin and Ellen until the mid-1950s when Ellen entered a care facility due to complications of Parkinson's disease.

The family appears to have prospered no better in Lincoln than in Grant, Sharon Springs, or Olney Springs. Edwin Origen's father died in 1933, and as the only child, he would have inherited his father's entire estate. His mother predeceased his father. Edwin Zenis's estate may have been considerable by today's standards. The money from the sale of the Grant farm was just a part of it. As a long-time employee of the railroad, Edwin Zenis might have accumulated significant assets. But apparently these assets did not do well after being passed to his son.

A family mystery surrounds the nomadic wanderings of Edwin and Ellen. Why would a couple who had sold a farm for more than $18,000 end up living for two or three years in a deserted sod house on the Kansas prairie? An amount of $18,500 in 1917 is equivalent to more than $340,000 in 2016. It seems likely that the Grant farm was always held in the name of his father, Edwin Zenis, and that Edwin Origen was obliged to return the amount of the purchase to his father and make his own way forward. If this interpretation is in fact true, it bespeaks nothing so much as an ungenerous attitude of father toward his only child.

Whatever those feelings might have been, it is at least objectively true that the Edwin Zenis family was, at one time, a family of not insignificant means. The estate in the early 1920s would be valued – in 2016 dollars – at approximately a half-million dollars. But by the late 1930s, the family of Edwin Origen Glass lived near the poverty line.

The Great Depression coupled with bad loans to family members and bad investments probably cost the families most of their wealth, and left the five sons pretty much on their own to make their way in the world. Edwin Origen is listed as having the occupation of janitor in the Lincoln City Directory throughout the 1930s, 1940s, and 1950s.

Edwin Origen Glass died on July 5, 1960, in Grand Island, Nebraska, of a burst aorta. He resided at that time with his son Gayland and daughter-in-law Helen Baerenbach Glass.

KENNETH LYLE FROST
(1909 – 2003; < Milton David < Sarah < Zenas)
GENERATION 12

Kenneth, the son of Milton David Frost & Belle Ann Frost, was born on May 20, 1890, in Blue Springs, Nebraska. In 1930, Kenneth was living in Oakland, California, in the household of his parents and was married to Edna M. Frost, who was born in Canada. In 1941, he was working as a railroad man in Oakland, California.

From his obituary, we learn that Kenneth lived to an advanced age:

> "Kenneth Lyle Frost, 94, of Crystal River, passed away June 5, 2003. He was a retired locomotive engineer, in which trade he served for 37 years. In addition to his current wife, Alice Frost, and daughter, Darlene, he is survived by his former wife, Mary C. King (married on January 12, 1936), of St. Augustine, their two daughters, Belle Ann Frost Cramer, Gresham, Ore., and Jackalyn Frost Schillig, Ponte Vedra Beach; eight grandchildren and 15 great grandchildren."

CLAUDE T. FROST
(1901 – 1963; < Milton D. < Sarah < Zenas)
GENERATION 12

Claude was born on November 5, 1901, in Wyoming. In 1941, he was working as a railroad brakeman in Oakland, California. He married Gussie Leota Heffelfinger, who was Swiss. Claude and Gussie had a daughter and two sons: Milton B. Frost (Generation 13), who was born in 1923, and Paul Eugene Frost (Generation 13), born in 1929. Milton B. Frost married Dorothy A. Runnells in Los Angeles, California, on June 24, 1950. In 1965, Milton was employed at Jack Frost Automotive (207 Lincoln Ave.) in San Jose, California. Paul Eugene Frost died on July 22, 2010, in Independence, Missouri. Betty P. Frost (Generation 13) was born in Nebraska in 1924. Nothing more is known of her life.

Claude died on June 6, 1963 in Fresno, California.

Glass Family in America

RODERICK JOSEPH FROST
(1923 – 1999; < Reuben O. < Sarah < Zenas)
GENERATION 12

"Rod" was a lifetime resident of Council Bluffs, Iowa. He graduated from St. Francis High school in 1941 and served in the U.S. Army during World War II, receiving the bronze star. He worked for Union Pacific Railroad for 40 years, retiring in 1983. He was a member of St. Peter's Church and Union Pacific Old Timers. He and his wife, Kathleen (Doyle) were married 51 years.

Their children are Madeline Shadden of Council Bluffs; Roderick "Rick" P. Frost of Ocean View, Hawaii. Roderick and Kathleen had five grandchildren.

EDWIN ORVILLE GLASS
(1909 – 1994; < Edwin Origen < Edwin Zenis < Zenas)
GENERATION 12

Edwin Orville Glass was born on August 24, 1909, in Grant, Nebraska. He was known as "Orville" all his life. (The name Orville appears no other place in the Glass family tree; its frequent use in the early 1900s is accounted for by the popularity of the Wright brothers, Orville and Wilbur.) Even before his grandfather's death in 1933, Edwin Origen's son Orville had to leave school after the 8th grade to help support the family. Edwin Origen supported the family as a house painter and later as a janitor. Orville was forthcoming in later years with his feelings of resentment against his father for having mismanaged an inheritance. There was property and other assets that ended up in the pockets of lawyers and businessmen. Orville sold newspapers and eventually apprenticed as a printer at the local newspaper while his siblings worked their way through elementary and secondary school.

Glass Family in America

Sometime shortly before 1929, Orville met **Grace Virginia Lintt** (see BRIEF BIOGRAPHIES). Orville and Grace were married on December 19, 1929, at their residence (2611 Y St.) in Lincoln, just two months after the stock market crash that signaled the beginning of the Great Depression. Nor did the family economy fare well during the first several years of marriage.

Orville finished his apprenticeship as a printer on June 1, 1931. He received his journeyman card on November 11, 1931. On April first of 1932, Orville and Grace moved to live with Orville's parents and siblings at 4104 G Street in Lincoln. Orville's siblings Victor and Gayland, at least, would have been resident in the G Street house at that time.

The couple's first child, Edwin Gordon, was born on October 22, 1932. A family of three probably lived less comfortably than a family of two, all the more so since Orville's employment at the newspaper was spotty during the Depression and due to his health problems. Nonetheless, they were able to purchase a residence at 4214 Lenox St. on March 15, 1934. A year later, another move took them to 4619 Hillside in College View, where they resided for one year before moving back to Lenox St. to reside with Grace's parents at 4220, the Lintt family home for several decades thereafter.

Either Orville was born with a kidney abnormality – both kidneys on one side of the spine – or his kidney was injured by horse kick as a boy. The former less adventurous story seems more likely. On December 30, 1936, Orville underwent an operation to remove one of his kidneys. His health history kept him out of military service when he and his four brothers traveled to Omaha to enlist after the Japanese attack on Pearl Harbor. That he was one two brothers not to serve in WWII was a source of embarrassment to Orville throughout much of his adult life.

Work was impossible for several months after the kidney operation. He was hospitalized for six weeks after the operation, compounded by a ruptured appendix. On May 9, 1937, the family of three moved to the Lintt family farm in Bennet, some 20 miles southeast of Lincoln. Grace told stories years later of picking sorrel, lambs quarters, and dandelion greens to supplement the family diet. These might appear on modern, toney restaurant menus as "Field Greens"; they were surely not regarded as delicacies during the Great Depression in Nebraska.

Orville secured work again at the Lincoln Journal newspaper, probably in late 1937. At that time, the family resided at 1531 North Cotner in the suburb of Bethany, Lincoln, Nebraska. Within eight months, they moved again to 6703 Holdrege, only a block away from the North Cotner apartment. The couple's second child, Ellen Gay, was born at Bryan Memorial Hospital on October 17, 1938, while the family of four resided at the Holdrege address.

Within a year of Ellen's birth, Grace was pregnant again. (Although she would not have known she was pregnant until sometime late in 1939 or early 1940, Grace was an indefatigable diarist who recorded the most mundane happenings in her life.)

Gene V Glass was born on June 19, 1940. The arrival of a third child so soon after the second, so soon after having survived the Great Depression, and at the dawn of the Second World War, must not have been a welcome event. It is said that Orville, at Grace's urging – or perhaps, insistence – received a vasectomy before the arrival of the third child. Vasectomies were not common in the 1940s. Moreover, Grace confessed decades later to one of her daughters-in-law that she tried several times to abort the pregnancy – by sitting in nearly scalding hot bath water, by jumping off ladders, and the like.

On October 8, 1943, the family moved from 67th & Holdrege to 6943 Lexington Avenue in the community of Bethany. The house was purchased for $600, which is equivalent in 2016 dollars to $8,000. The family resided there until 1948, shortly before which time Orville and

Grace bought a "drug store"[25] in the 1500 block of North Cotner Blvd. in Bethany. Orville continued to work as a printer at the newspaper while Grace managed the drug store. The store was open from 8 am until 10 pm seven days a week, and remained so for 11 years. Orville would join Grace in managing the store after work at the *Lincoln Journal* and a shower. The store was never closed a single day in eleven years and even transacted business when the fire fighters visited the apartment above the store to put out a kitchen fire. (That apartment, incidentally, was sometimes visited by Charles Starkweather, the infamous mass murderer of 11 persons in the winter of 1957-8 in Lincoln, in Wyoming, and on a farm adjacent to Grace's parents' farm in Bennett.)

Within a year of acquiring the drug store on December 5, 1948, Orville and Grace bought the two-story apartment building three doors south of the store at 1529 No. Cotner Blvd. The family – Orville, Grace, Ellen, Gene, and Edwin for two or three years – resided there together or in part for the next 35 years.

One vivid memory of your chronicler involves the North Cotner residence, Edwin Gordon Glass, and our mother. As may be recalled, Orville, Grace and Edwin lived in the apartment at 1529 North Cotner from August 1937 to May 1938. This apartment was on the second floor of the building that they purchased in December 1948, and occupied in one configuration or another for more than 30 years. So the family resided again at 1529 North Cotner in 1950. Edwin was 5 years old in September 1938, and was 18 years old in September 1950. Grace stood at the front door in September 1950 and bade goodbye to Ed as he left for his first year of college at Nebraska Wesleyan University. She turned back to the living room, where I sat, and wiped a tear from her eye. I asked her why she was crying, and she said that 18 years before, she had

---

[25] In the 1940s and 1950s, the distinction between "pharmacies" and "drug stores" was not generally nor carefully observed. In part, this was due to the relative lack of tested and approved pharmaceuticals and the widespread use of "over the counter" or patent medicines. The Glass Confectionery employed no certified pharmacist, but it was known in the community as a "drug store."

waved goodbye to her son, Edwin, as he departed from that very same location to travel across the street for his first day in Kindergarten at Bethany Elementary School. So much had happened to the family in those 18 years: loss, pain, poverty, war, births, some deaths, unemployment, and a tiny measure of prosperity born of hard work.

Ellen and Gene's teen years centered around the store, the schools across the street (Bethany Elementary), or a mile north (Northeast Junior and Senior High School). The family seldom dined together at home. Many meals were taken at Shorty's Cafe next to the drug store. (Your chronicler's taste for cheeseburgers, chili, white gravy, and canned corn probably stems from those years.)

Glass Confectionery, the so-called drug store, was sold in about 1960. Grace retired while Orville continued to work as a printer, then at the Nebraska Salesbook Co. His union, the International Typographical Union, struck against his employer in 1963, in protest of the appearance of computers in the composing room. Orville performed his duties on the picket line, but never worked another day at the trade that supported his family for more than thirty years. When he subsequently retired, the ITU pension fund was broke, the printing trade having been completely wiped out by computers.

Although retired, without a pension, and employed at odd jobs for a few years, Orville's habit of saving and his smart investing managed to maintain himself and his spouse in comfortable, if not, extravagant circumstances the rest of their lives. As a retiree, he was able to indulge his passion for horse racing, even to the extent of acquiring a couple of race horses and racing them in tracks around Nebraska and Iowa.

Orville and Grace "wintered" for several months in McAllen, Texas, for a few years in the middle 1960s. Orville was a fan of horse racing nearly all his adult life. In the late 1960s, he acquired a couple of horses and raced them in Nebraska, South Dakota, and Colorado.

Glass Family in America

As was mentioned above, Grace kept a diary from the 1930s until she lost all command of language in the late 1970s. She wrote a clearly legible hand and her spelling and grammar were impeccable. Grace was an intelligent woman; she graduated from Lincoln High School in 1929, where she played second violin in a very accomplished orchestra. All her adult life she enjoyed solving crossword puzzles and playing word games. She loved Scrabble. But beginning in the early 1970s and continuing for about five years, the entries in her diaries deteriorated. A word might be misspelled or a rebus might be substituted for a word that could no longer be recalled. Her final entries around 1980 were simply numbers: 189, 32-14, 86, and the like. Orville later explained that these entries were figures seen on television during a football game, or readings from the car's odometer. The plaque was slowly eradicating Grace's ability to understand words and was working its way to the number section of the brain.

Orville cared for Grace at home as long as he possibly could, motivated perhaps as much by his love for his spouse as by his concern about money and his dread of living alone. A few years before her death, he moved her to a nursing home in Ashland, Nebraska, some 25 miles from Bethany. He visited her daily and participated actively in her care. Grace died on May 10, 1986, at the age of 74 from what was probably Alzheimer's disease. Her descent was excruciatingly slow, having taken more than 10 years.

Orville took his meals after Grace's move to Ashland at a café in the 1500 block of North Cotner. There he made the acquaintance of a cook and waitress named Lou Rose. Lou was a widow and was well known in the area for her pies. They struck up a relationship and it was not long before Orville sold the apartment building and moved in with Lou at her home at 60th Street and Judson, about two miles north of Bethany. The year was 1982.

Orville and Lou lived together for the next 12 years. She was a charming, gracious, and understanding partner, by all appearances. Orville and Lou may have been a better match than Orville and Grace, but no one has the perspective nor the experience to judge such things. However, few would gainsay the claim that Lou Rose was a wonderful partner to Orville Glass in the last decade of his life. Orville developed colo-rectal cancer at about age 70 and was treated surgically for it. He died on October 13, 1994, in Bryan Memorial Hospital at Lincoln from complications of surgery for esophageal cancer.

Orville filed his last will and testament on July 7, 1978. It left his entire estate to his wife, Grace Virginia Glass. Since Grace predeceased him, the estate then was left to his three children in equal amounts. In April, 1995, when his estate was distributed, it was worth approximately $280,000. The purchasing power of $280,000 in 1995 is equal to $440,000 in 2016. For a man who left school in the 8th grade to help support his father's family, who was unemployed for several years during the Great Depression, and who lived simply and frugally when times were better, to have left an estate of almost a half million dollars was a noteworthy achievement. Before he died, Orville retired the mortgage, supplied an automobile, and otherwise provided for the future of his domestic partner, Lou Rose.

MILTON COLLINS GLASS
(1911 – 1968 ; < Edwin Origen < Edwin Zenis < Zenas)
GENERATION 12

Milton (or Buzz as he was known) was born in Grant, Nebraska, on May 30, 1911, the second child of Edwin Origen and Nora Ellen Glass. Throughout his childhood he lived in Grant, Sharon Springs, Kansas, Olney Springs, Colorado, and Lincoln, Nebraska. He married Eleanor Idamae Hilliard (See BRIEF BIOGRAPHIES) in Lincoln. In the mid-1940s, Milton and his wife moved to California, where he worked as a printer. In the words of his daughter-in-law, Teri Eldridge, wife of son Paul, Buzz was a quiet, uncomplaining man who worked very hard, often at two jobs, to provide for his parents and later for his family. He is remembered by his nephew, Edwin Gordon Glass, as being extremely taciturn. His hobby as a young man was keeping racing pigeons.

Buzz and Ida had three sons: **Philip Roy** (1942), **Paul Raymond** (born 1947) and Glenn Russell Glass (born 1952). All three sons were born in California. Milton died at the relatively early age of 57 on October 20, 1968, in Alhambra, California, of metastasized cancer. Like his older brother Edwin Orville, Buzz was

Glass Family in America

employed as a printer during his adult life. A common chemical used for cleaning in the printing trade was Methyl Ethyl Ketone (commercial name Butanone). Butanone is now known to have adverse effects on the health of persons in regular contact with it.

The family settled first in Temple City, California, from 1948 to 1952. While at the **Temple City** residence, Buzz's brother Victor and his new wife Gladys moved to California and lived briefly with Buzz and Ida while they were finding a place to live. Later Buzz and his family moved to La Puente from 1952 until 1964.

LYLE CALVIN GLASS
(1913 – 1996 ; Edwin Origen < Edwin Zenis < Zenas)
GENERATION 12

Lyle Calvin Glass (pictured with his sister **Eva Ann Glass**) was born in Grant, Nebraska, on November 20, 1913, the third son of Edwin Origen and Nora Ellen Glass. He married Blanche Davis (see BRIEF BIOGRAPHIES) in Lincoln, Nebraska. Lyle enlisted in the Army in July, 1942. He was trained as a radio mechanic at Scott Field in Belleville, Illinois, and he was sent overseas in November, 1942, the first of the brothers to serve outside the U.S. Blanche lived in Miami, Florida, while Lyle was in service. After being discharged from the Army at the end of the war, Lyle and Blanche remained in Florida, where they made their home the rest of their lives. They adopted a son named Clint Lyle Glass. Lyle Calvin died March 29, 1996, in Ocklawaha, Florida.

VICTOR BUREN GLASS
(1920 – 1994 ; < Edwin Origen < Edwin Zenis < Zenas)
(Generation 12)

Born in Sharon Springs, Kansas, on September 18, 1920. Vic was raised in Lincoln, Nebraska. He graduated from Lincoln High School in about 1938.

Vic served in Europe during WWII, having been inducted into the Army in February, 1942, and was honorably discharged in 1946 at the rank of Tech Sergeant. His service in the European theater included participation in the second wave of troops invading Normandy in 1944 and in the Battle of the Bulge from December, 1944, to January, 1945, some six weeks. The Battle of the Bulge was the fiercest hostility of WWII for the U.S. Some 10,000 American troops were killed and tens of thousands suffered injuries. Victor suffered repeated trauma as a result of the battle and took a significant period of time to recover after discharge. Family lore has it that Vic was wounded in these battles and kept the fact a secret for a long time so as not to worry his parents.

He married Gladys Annette Davis from Burchard, Nebraska, on October 13, 1947. Vic and Gladys had two children: Gary Dean and **Virginia Ann**. The family lived in La Puente, California, for many years where Vic worked in the aircraft industry. Gladys died in 1973. He spent his later years with his son, Gary, in Ogden, Utah. He died on July 2, 1994 in Ogden, Utah, and is buried there in the Evergreen Memorial Park. Gary died in 1995 soon after his father, having suffered a malignant brain tumor.

WARREN GAYLAND GLASS
(1920 – 2005; < Edwin Origen < Edwin Zenis < Zenas)
GENERATION 12

Gayland was born in Olney Springs, Colorado, on February 20, 1920. He was raised throughout most of his youth in Lincoln, Nebraska. He graduated from Lincoln High School in 1940. Gayland was an accomplished baseball player; he pitched and was left-handed. He had a brief career in semi-pro baseball and was invited to try out for the Boston Red Sox. His baseball career was interrupted by WW II.

Gayland enlisted in the Navy on July 31, 1942. From March, 1943, to January, 1945, he served on the U.S.S. Daley, a destroyer, in the 7th Fleet under the command of Admiral Kinkaid. Most of this time was spent in the Pacific theater. The 7th Fleet supported MacArthur's campaign to regain control of the Philippines. His ship participated in some 15 hostilities in the Pacific Theater. He spent January to June 1945 at the Norfolk, Virginia Naval Base, and served for five months on the U.S.S. Burdo until being discharged on October 31, 1945.

Gayland married **Helen Virginia Baerenbach** (See BRIEF BIOGRAPHIES) in New York, NY, on June 24, 1943, while he was on a six-day leave, from the Brooklyn Navy Yards. His brother Victor attended as best man. Helen was attended by her cousin, Lillian Nehr. Helen's parents gave the couple a gift of $500; other relatives contributed $150, and Helen opened a bank account for the couple in the amount of $700. Gayland and Helen moved to Lincoln, Nebraska, in the late 1940s after he had worked for a

short while at Bloomingdales department store in Manhattan. He was employed by Sears Roebuck in Lincoln and Grand Island, Nebraska, throughout the 1950s and 1960s. The couple relocated to Lakewood, Colorado, in the 1970s. During the 1970s, Helen worked as a teacher's aide and Gayland was office manager for a medical practice. In the 1990s, they resided in Escondido, California.

Gayland never had children. In WW II, he served in the engine room of a destroyer. He was subjected to long periods of extreme heat. It is likely that he suffered from oligospermia (low sperm count) as a result. The couple's desire for a child may have been satisfied by their close relationship with the daughters of their neighbors in Lakewood, Colorado. The Beglers had three daughters, one of whom is Jamie. Helen and Gayland always spoke fondly of their little girl, Jamie. Jamie is currently Dr. Jamie Begler Houg, an MD in internal medicine, practicing in Littleton, Colorado.

Gayland died on June 9, 2005, and is buried at Fort Logan Military Cemetery in Lakewood, Colorado. Helen died at age 93 on July 5, 2016, in an assisted living residence in Parker, Colorado. Lynda Begler, her neighbor from Lakewood, Colorado, assisted greatly in making the decisions that made Helen's advanced years as comfortable as was possible. Helen's death marked the end of the generation of the five Glass brothers and their widows, a period of 107 years.

EVA ANN GLASS
(1926 – 1936 ; < Edwin Origen < Edwin Zenis < Zenas)
GENERATION 12

Eva Ann (or "Eve-Ann" as she was known to her family during her brief lifetime) was born on June 10, 1926, as the sixth child and only daughter of Edwin Origen and Nora Ellen Glass. She lived her whole life in Lincoln, Nebraska. She died on June 28, 1936, as the result of an appendectomy operation. Julie Evann Glass, daughter of Gene V Glass and Sharon Lea Grossoehme, born on October 18, 1963, was named after Eva Ann.

1950 THE DIASPORA

> A **diaspora** (from Greek διασπορά, "scattering, dispersion") is a scattered population whose origin lies within a smaller geographic locale. (Wikipedia)

Up until the mid-20th century, the Somerset Glass(e) family in America could be traced to only a few locations: the Boston area, Connecticut, Vermont, New York State, Pennsylvania, Michigan, western Illinois, and Nebraska. But the effects of WW II and the rise of corporations and nationwide organizations scattered the Glass family across the entire U.S. By the early 21st century, the descendants of the four Glass(e) siblings from Somerset, England, could be found in most of the 50 states.

RODERICK PAUL FROST
(1950 – 2013; < Roderick J. < Reuben O. < Sarah)
Generation 13

Sarah (Glass) Frost's great-grandson, Roderick, was born in 1950 in Council Bluffs, Iowa. He was a medical technician at the Veterans Administration Hospital of Omaha. He was also an active volunteer in the Ocean View, Hawaii community and a U.S. Air Force veteran. Roderick died July 15, 2013, at Kona Community Hospital. He was survived by a son, Roderick James Frost, of Omaha, Nebraska; daughters, Kathy Kruskamp of Spearfish, South Dakota; Jessica Rieser and Cassandra Frost of Omaha, Nebraska, and five grandchildren.

EDWIN GORDON GLASS
(1932 –   ; Edwin Orville < Edwin Origen< Edwin Zenis)
GENERATION 13

Edwin Gordon Glass – son of Edwin Orville Glass, grandson of Edwin Origen Glass, and who was known variously as Sonny, Bosco, or Ed throughout his lifetime – was born October 22, 1932, in Lincoln, Nebraska. He was educated at Bethany Elementary School and Northeast Junior and Senior High School. He entered Nebraska Wesleyan University in the fall of 1950.

On August 10, 1951, he married Mary Lou Sabin (See BRIEF BIOGRAPHIES) at the St. Paul Methodist Church in University Place adjacent to the NWU campus. Ed and Mary Lou had been "steadies" for about three years at the time of their wedding. Mary Lou took employment at the telephone company as a secretary – having mastered both touch-typing and shorthand in high school – to support Ed's postsecondary education. The couple resided at various locations in the University Place and Bethany communities during the first several months of their marriage.

The couple's life was blessed with the arrival of their first child, Gregory Scott Glass, on August 27, 1954. Their second and third children arrived soon after: Karen Sue Glass was born June 16, 1956, and Zachary Alan Glass, on September 18, 1958.

Although Ed's college education prepared him for a career as a high school history teacher, upon graduation he chose instead to take employment as a YMCA (Young Men's Christian Association) director. His first assignment was as director of the Northeast Lincoln YMCA, but he soon assumed the position of Director for the main YMCA facility in downtown Lincoln. During the decade of the 1950s and early 1960s, the family resided in several locations, including adjacent to the Lintt family home on Lenox Street, Huntington Avenue near 63rd Street, and in the 6900 block of Colby Street, one block north of the Orville Glass family's former residence on Lexington Avenue.

Edwin Gordon held the position of Director of the Northeast Lincoln YMCA from 1956 to 1959; he assumed Directorship of the main Lincoln YMCA until 1963 when he assumed the position as Director of the Littleton, Colorado YMCA. After a ten-year tenure as Director of the Littleton YMCA, a position he held until 1967. Ed was tapped to head the downtown Denver YMCA in 1967, which position he held for 13 years. In 1980, he was appointed Director of metropolitan Oklahoma City YMCA, and he and Mary Lou moved to Edmond, OK, a suburb of Oklahoma City. He retired from YMCA work in 1993. After retirement, he took up residence in Parker, Colorado, a suburb south of Denver. He continued to work with the YMCA national office as a consultant to local Ys, having served more than 50 local organizations before final retirement in about 2005. In about 2005, Ed and Mary Lou acquired a property in Sun Lakes, Arizona, a suburb southeast of Phoenix. At this point – 2016 – they split their time between Parker and Sun Lakes.

Edwin Gordon and Edwin Orville Glass (circa 1990)

Ed is an accomplished golfer, having taken up the sport early in life and dedicated many years to perfecting his game. He holds the distinction of having "shot his age" on the golf course, not just once but hundreds of times. This is an accomplishment so rare that no statistics are available on the percentage of golfers who ever attain the goal. Perhaps only one in one million golfers ever breaks their age, but this could be a gross underestimate; it could easily be one in two million.

ELLEN GAY GLASS
(1938 –   ; Orville < Edwin Origen< Edwin Zenis)
GENERATION 13

Ellen Gay Glass – daughter of Edwin Orville Glass, granddaughter of Edwin Origen Glass – was born on October 17, 1938, in Lincoln at Bryan Memorial Hospital. Her middle name probably derives from that of her uncle, Gayland Warren Glass. She was raised in the Lincoln suburb of Bethany, and was educated at Bethany Elementary School and **Northeast Junior and Senior High School**, one year, 1956 -1957 at Nebraska Wesleyan University, and at the University of Nebraska, 1974 - 1980. In 1956, Ellen was reintroduced to Warren Clements Spence who had moved back to Lincoln from California. The Spence and Glass families shared a very long and close friendship. Warren was thirteen years Ellen's senior; it was an old but new relationship. On June 25, 1958, Warren and Ellen were married in North Platte, Nebraska. Warren's sister Elizabeth and her husband, George King, stood with the couple in a private wedding. Warren died in 2014, at age 87 after 55 years of marriage, from complications of heart disease, multiple cancers, and dementia. (See BRIEF BIOGRAPHIES.)

At the time of their marriage, **Warren** had recently gained employment with the U.S. Postal Service, where he worked until retirement, in 1986. Ellen and Warren's only child, Leonard Dean Spence, was born on April 2, 1959. Ellen, Warren, and Leonard resided in the vicinity of Bethany for more than 50 years. For 25 years, they resided at 1425 No. 65th Street.

Ellen worked for Pamida, a department store, in Bethany, a suburb of Lincoln, from 1976 to 1984. She served in the capacity of secretary at the Nebraska Soybean Board from 1990 to 1996. She worked for the Nebraska Department of Revenue from 1997 to 2000.

GENE V GLASS
(1940 –   ; Orville < Edwin Origen< Edwin Zenis)
GENERATION 13

Gene V Glass was born on June 19, 1940. Apparently there was some disagreement between his parents over what his name would be. His siblings had been given names after Orville's family names: Edwin and Ellen. But Grace, perhaps still unhappy about such a quick pregnancy after Ellen's birth, rejected any suggestion by Orville of another name taken from his family history. Grace insisted on the name Gene – the name of a former boyfriend – and she wanted the new baby's initials to match hers: GVG for Grace Virginia Glass. So Orville suggested the middle name Victor, after his next to youngest brother, Victor Buren. Grace rejected that suggestion and insisted that the new baby have no middle name, simply the letter V. And so it was.

Gene attended **Bethany Elementary** and Northeast Junior and Senior High School, as did his siblings. He spent two years at Nebraska Wesleyan University, and three semesters at the University of Nebraska in Lincoln before being accepted to graduate school at the University of Wisconsin in Madison, Wisconsin, in the fall of 1961. He finished graduate school in May, 1965.

Gene married his girlfriend of several years, Sharon Lea Grossoehme, (see BRIEF BIOGRAPHIES), at the St. Paul Methodist Church in University Place, Lincoln, on August 16, 1959.

Their daughter, Julie Evann Glass, was born at 10 p.m. on October 18, 1963, at Madison (Wisconsin) General Hospital. The family moved to Champaign, Illinois, in August of 1965, when Gene accepted a job at the University of Illinois. They resided in Illinois for two years until the family relocated to Boulder, Colorado, in connection with Gene's appointment to the faculty of the University of Colorado.

Gene and Sharon separated on October 31, 1974, and were divorced on August 18, 1975. Gene had a house built at 1735 Gillaspie Drive in Boulder and occupied it with Mary Lee Smith in June, 1975 (See BRIEF BIOGRAPHIES). In February, 1975, Gene was elected President of the American Educational Research Association, the youngest person to attain that office in the 110-year history of the Association. Gene and Mary Lee were married by a Unitarian minister at the Gillaspie Drive residence on June 19, 1977, with Gene's parents, daughter Julie, brother and sister-in-law Ed and Mary Lou and their three children, and friend Marilyn Averill present. In 1978, the couple moved to 1006 6th Street in Boulder.

The marriage between Gene Glass and Mary Lee Smith ended in divorce in 1991, while the couple lived at 3031 60th Street in Phoenix, Arizona, where the couple lived after accepting appointments to the faculty of Arizona State University in August, 1986.

Gene lived with Sandra Jo Golner (nee Rubin, see BRIEF BIOGRAPHIES) in Scottsdale while Sandy finished her doctoral degree. Sandy graduated with a PhD in Education Policy in May, 1993, the same month in which Gene converted to Judaism and in which he and Sandy were married in the yard adjoining their home in the community of Spanish Oaks in Scottsdale. The ceremony was conducted by Rabbi Charles Herring. In attendance were many of the bride and groom's families: The groom's father and Lou Rose; the bride's parents Lorraine and Lawrence Rubin, both the bride and groom's siblings and children, Gayland and Helen Glass, and many friends.

Gene and Sandy moved to **Colonia Encantada at 7500 E. McCormick Parkway** in 1995, having made a down payment on their new residence with the $70,000 left to them in Orville Glass's will. After residing part of the year at various locations in Boulder, Colorado, while still working at Arizona State

University during the academic year, in 2009 they purchased a residence at **2920 Lafayette Drive in Boulder**, tore it down, and rebuilt a home that was completed four or five years later. After Gene and Sandy's retirement in 2010, they lived winters in Scottsdale, Arizona, and summers in Boulder, Colorado.

Some will read these pages searching for information about what genetic influences might have been passed on that will affect one's health. That is a perfectly understandable basis for being interested in genealogy.

Gene was treated for prostate cancer in 2005; he suffered a heart attack in the spring of 2009, which resulted in the placement of three stents and a pacemaker; he was diagnosed with non-Hodgkins follicular lymphoma in 2013, was treated for the same until August 2015, and was in remission thereafter until the time of this writing.

PHILIP ROY GLASS (1942 –   )
(1942 –   ; Milton Collins < Edwin Origen < Edwin Zenis)
GENERATION 13

Phil Glass is the eldest son of Milton and Eleanor Idamae (Hilliard) Glass. He was born on October 21, 1942, in Alhambra, California. In 1944, he was brought to Lincoln, Nebraska, to meet his grandparents, uncles and aunts, and **cousins Gene and Ellen Glass**.

From 1952 until 1964, the family lived in **La Puente, California**. He married Wilma J. Wade on December 31, 1966, in Covina, California. He later married Malinda S. Moulton on September 1, 1973, in Los Angeles. Malinda brought a daughter, Carrie Moulton, into the marriage. The second marriage lasted four years.

In about 1980, Phil married Karen D. Dayley-Burnett who had three daughters, Kayleen, Christine, and Kimberly by Kenneth Burnett to whom Karen had been sealed in the Mormon Temple in Salt Lake City. Kenneth died in 1979 of cancer. Karen was born on December 29, 1945, in Ogden, Utah. They were married in Ogden and immediately returned to LaVerne, California, where Phil had a home. After some time, they sold their holdings there and purchased a ranch in Roy, Utah. Phil and Karen's two children were both born while the couple lived in LaVerne, California: Jason C. Glass, born on March 2, 1982, and Katie D. Glass, born January 17, 1987.

Phil served as a medic in the armed forces. He started his civilian career in the automotive racing industry. He then branched out into sales and photography, filling government contracts for special research & development weaponry and devices. (e.g., Starlight Scopes and the like) In retirement, Phil works on restoring classic cars and tractors.

In 2016, Phil and Karen were living in Roy, Utah.

Glass Family in America

Phil, Glenn and Paul Glass in 1974, San Dimas, California

PAUL RAYMOND GLASS
(1947 –   ; Milton Collins < Edwin Origen < Edwin Zenis)
GENERATION 13

Paul grew up in La Puente, California, and moved with the family to Glendora, California, in 1963. He attended La Puente schools for most of his education but transferred in the middle of his sophomore year and then graduated from Glendora High School.

Glass Family in America

Paul's first job at age 13 was sweeping the parking lot of a small grocery store around the corner from his home. As he grew older a neighbor was able to help him get a job at a larger grocery store, Covina Farms, where he bagged potatoes. In Paul's later teen years, he worked at 76-Union Gas Station pumping gas, changing oil, and washing windshields. His good friend, Larry VanVliet also worked at the gas station - Larry was the best man at Paul's wedding as well as his life long friend. Paul's brother, Phil, ran around with a racing crowd that included the Belanger brothers, Jerry and Bob (Gaston). The Belanger's had a "header shop" that needed welders and tube-benders. Paul thought that sounded like interesting work so he left the service station for greener pastures. (The Belanger family moved their business from Covina, CA, and ended up in Peoria, AZ, where they still do business in 2016.)

At this stage in his life, Paul developed an interest in law enforcement and took college courses at Mt. San Antonio College in Walnut, California. Concurrently, his father Buzz became ill and the family was thrown into turmoil. Their Glendora home was sold, there were several moves and Buzz was in and out of the hospital. By the time the doctors were able to diagnose his ailments, his cancer was so far progressed that they gave him little hope of living much longer. Paul put his career/education plans on hold to help his mother and to take care of his younger brother Glenn. Phil, who had served as a medic in the Army and was not living with the family by this time, was instrumental in providing care for his father and relieving his mother of the full care-giving burden.

Following his father's death in 1968, Paul stayed with his mother Idamae and younger brother. He took a job with Crippen Ambulance Company in Covina, and they rented a house in downtown Covina from Clyde George Baldosser, who figured in important ways in Idamae's future.

Paul had continued to stay in contact with his friends from Glendora High School. It was through those contacts that he met Teri Eldridge, his future wife, and learned that she had lived just up the street from his former Glendora home.

Paul married **Therese Pauline Eldridge** (see BRIEF BIOGRAPHIES) on Saturday, October 23, 1971, at the Sacred Heart Chapel in Covina. She was born at Edwards Air Force Base, California, on May 4, 1952, to Donald Edward Eldridge and Charlotte Viviane Fortin-Eldridge; her father was English and her mother was French.

When they first married, Paul and Teri lived in an apartment in Covina just around the corner from Paul's brother Phil. At the time, Teri, 19 years old, was in her third year of college, working for Bank of America as a teller and NCR Proof Machine Operator. Paul began working for the State of California, Department of Transportation. Within a year they purchased a four-bedroom house in San Dimas, California. Initially, they both continued to work but when their first child Aimee arrived in the summer of 1974, they made the decision that Teri should stay at home and be a full-time homemaker. Paul continued to earn promotions within the Department of Transportation and became a Heavy Equipment Operator. He took night classes at Citrus College and at UCLA. Two years later their second daughter, Anne Marie, was born. With another promotion for Paul, they purchased a home in Big Bear, California, and enjoyed the mountain life for two years. Continuing his education and training allowed Paul to consistently advance through the ranks. Taking another promotion, he moved his family to Calimesa, California, near Idamae and family. His final promotion was to head of budgets and contracts for the North and South Regions for CalTrans District 8, California, Department of Transportation's largest district.

Paul came to faith in Christ through the influence of his wife Teri. The whole family attends a non-denominational, Bible teaching church in Yucaipa, California. Paul and Teri attend Sunday services regularly and meet mid-week with a small group of friends from church for fellowship and Bible study. A regular habit for Teri, Paul has found the fellowship to be a fun addition to his retirement years. A rather shy man with a wild sense of humor, Paul has always enjoyed motor sports, particularly motorcycles. His current ride is a sedate Honda Silverwing 600 cc Mega Beast - Scooter. In addition to all motor sports (speed way, moto-cross, Isle of Man races, drag races, and the like) Paul is a gentleman farmer keeping hens for eggs, manning a moderate size goldfish pond, growing vegetables and fruit, camping in his pop-up trailer, keeping in contact with his current friends and his friends from the La Puente and Glendora days, and spending time with his grandsons. His first dog was a loving beast of a Great Dane named Tahoe that he brought into the marriage and his current pet is an equally devoted 95 lb. Golden-doodle named Ziva.

In regard to health issues, Paul has had repeated issues with calcium based stag-horned kidney stones and some skin cancers from sun exposure. Following retirement Paul experienced an irregular heartbeat. At first the doctors thought his heart might be preparing for a heart attack but upon closer examination found that the severe arrhythmias he was experiencing were a result of misfires in the right and left atrium of the heart's control center. Once he was given the proper doses of magnesium and potassium as well as a medication that seems to be working for him at this time, the doctors put off installing a pace-maker. Lastly, age has brought some arthritis and from his days of working with heavy equipment, before the time of ear-protection, Paul lives with significant hearing loss.

Paul and Teri have two daughters: **Aimee Kathleen Glass**, born on July 2, 1974, and **Anne Marie Glass**, born on July 1, 1976. They have seven grandsons.

Paul and Teri were living in Yucaipa, California, in 2016.

GLENN RUSSELL GLASS
(1952 –   ; Milton Collins < Edwin Origen < Edwin Zenis)
GENERATION 13

Glenn Russell Glass was born on January 30, 1957, to Milton Collins and Eleanor Idamae (Hilliard) Glass in Alhambra, California. Glenn's first name was suggested by his mother, who was an admirer of the screen actor, Glenn Ford. From 1964 to 1968, they family lived in **Glendora, California**. Glen married Shelly Belinda Ratcliff in June of 1980 at Calimesa, California. Shelly was born in San Bernardino, CA, on June 19, 1964. Their son Scott Chandler Glass was born on March 4, 1987, and adopted by Glenn and Shelly shortly thereafter.

Glenn first worked as a carpenter, then as a licensed contractor, throughout the Yucaipa/San Bernardino Valley in eastern California. In the early 1990s he moved his family to Lake Havasu City, Arizona, where he became the sole proprietor of a large bike shop, selling high-end bicycles, accessories, sponsoring BMX Racers and other local events. He also invested in real estate in the area. Shelly became a dental assistant and then a dental hygienist. Having their investments pay out well, they sold their Lake Havasu properties after some time and moved to Flagstaff, Arizona, where they were residing in 2016. Currently, Glenn manages several dental practices in Flagstaff, Shelly works as a hygienist, and Scott holds a license as a Registered Nurse.

CLINT LYLE GLASS
(1965 –   ; < Lyle Calvin < Edwin Origen < Edwin Zenis)
GENERATION 13

Clint Lyle Glass is the son of Lyle Calvin and Blanche (Davis) Glass. He was born on May 24, 1965, in Florida. He was adopted at birth by his parents, Lyle and Blanche. Clint graduated from Lake Weir High School in Ocala, Florida, in 1989. He married **Karen Boehmer** on October 14, 1989. Their daughter Kaylin Nicole was born March 3, 1993, in Ocala; their son, Colton Joshua Glass, was born May 31, 2007. Kaylin married Eric Corn Cornelison on August 23, 2015. In 2016, Clint was serving as District Manager for Republic National Distributing, a company with which he had worked since 1989.

GARY DEAN GLASS
(1948 – 1995; < Victor < Edwin Origen < Edwin Zenis)
GENERATION 13

Gary was born on December 5, 1948, in Lincoln, Nebraska. He was raised largely in the Los Angeles area, specifically, La Puente. He may have married Sharon A. Rasco in

Los Angeles on June 9, 1973. During his adult years, Gary and his family lived in Ogden, Utah. Little is known about his adult life. However, the headstone on his grave indicates that he served in Vietnam in the Air Force. His father Victor lived with him for the last years of his life. Gary died one year after his father on July 13, 1995, of a malignant brain tumor in Clearfield, Utah. It's not known if his service in the Vietnam War involved exposure to Agent Orange that may be linked to Glioblastoma Multiforme Stage 4 Brain Cancer.

VIRGINIA ANN GLASS
(1950 –   ; < Victor < Edwin Origen < Edwin Zenis)
GENERATION 13

We have lost track of Virginia. At one time she was believed to have been living in San Diego, California. A relative thought that she was married to a man from Michigan. Nothing more is known to this writer.

GREGORY SCOTT GLASS
(1954 –   ; < Edwin Gordon < Edwin Orville < Edwin Origen)
GENERATION 14

Greg Glass, the first son of Edwin Gordon and Mary Lou (Sabin) Glass was born on August 27, 1954, in Lincoln, Nebraska. Greg attended schools in Lincoln and in Littleton, Colorado, before graduating from Arapahoe High School in 1972. He attended college at the University of Southern Colorado at Pueblo in the mid-1970s, graduating with a degree in Education. Greg married Linda S. Buchholtz (see BRIEF BIOGRAPHIES) on May 13, 1978, in Denver, Colorado. Their union produced two sons: Jason Scott Glass, born on December 4, 1978, and Joshua Steven Glass, born on November 7, 1981.

On October 12, 2001, Greg married **Susan Martinez** in Honolulu, Hawaii (see BRIEF BIOGRAPHIES). In 2016, they reside in the Upper Bear Creek area of Evergreen, Colorado. Greg and Susan have traveled extensively. They have been to Europe a number of times, Central America, Canada, New Zealand.

KAREN SUE GLASS
(1956 –   ; < Edwin Gordon < Edwin Orville < Edwin Origen)
GENERATION 14

Karen Sue Glass, the daughter of Ed and Mary Lou Glass, was born on June 16, 1956, in Lincoln, Nebraska. Karen attended schools in Lincoln and in Littleton, Colorado, before graduating from Littleton High School in 1974. She attended college and received a Bachelor of Science degree in Nursing from the University of Colorado School of Medicine in 1979. Karen worked as a nurse at St. Anthony Hospital in Denver from 1980 to 1981.

Karen met **Jan Ryd** (see BRIEF BIOGRAPHIES) while doing restaurant work in the early 1980s. They were married on July 3, 1982, in Evergreen, Colorado. The couple resided in Evergreen for three years, then in Indian Hills for two years, and Conifer, Colorado, for seven years. They moved to Lakewood, Colorado, in 1994 and were residing there in 2016.

Karen started a home and commercial cleaning company called K's Cleaning Company in 1984. Both Karen and Jan ran the company until 2004 when they opened Lee Myles Autocare in Lakewood, Colorado. They operated both businesses until 2010 when they sold the cleaning business. In 2013, they opened Lee Myles Autocare in Northglen, Colorado, and in 2015, Lee Myles Autocare in Boulder, Colorado.

Karen and Jan have three children: Amanda, Erik, and Axel Gordon. Their son Erik works as the office manager at the Boulder establishment.

Glass Family in America

Gregory, Zachary, Edwin, and Mary Lou, Karen in 2016

ZACHARY ALAN GLASS
(1958 –   ; < Edwin Gordon < Edwin Orville < Edwin Origen)
GENERATION 14

Zachary Alan Glass is the second son of Edwin and Mary Lou Glass. He was born on September 18, 1958, in Lincoln, Nebraska. Zach attended elementary and secondary school in Littleton, Colorado, and graduated from Littleton High School in about 1976. Zach married Sandra Lee Hughes in 1985 in Denver. Sandy was born September 28, 1957, in Cleveland, Ohio. The family resided in Elizabeth, Colorado, for several years preceding 2016.

Zach and Sandy have twin boys: Kyle Lee Glass and Dane Alan Glass.

LEONARD DEAN SPENCE
(1959 –   ; < Ellen Gay < Edwin Orville < Edwin Origen)
GENERATION 14

Leonard Spence, the only child of Ellen Gay Glass and **Warren Spence**, was born in Lincoln, Nebraska, on April 2, 1959. He attended Bethany Elementary, and Mickle Junior High School, and attended Northeast High School. He attended Southeast Community College. He worked for Tri-Con, a motorcycle manufacturing company, and Lester Electrical Company. He was employed at Walmart from 2010 until 2015. He was employed at Bryan Health Center, East Campus, starting in 2015.

Leonard married **Eam Ath** (see BRIEF BIOGRAPHIES) on April 5, 1997, in Lincoln in a traditional church wedding and a Buddhist ceremony performed in their home. Leonard changed his name to Leo at the same time Eam gained her citizenship and was able to assume an American name, Amy. Eam is the daughter of Ath Bhy and Leoup Sor. She was born April 13, 1966, in Battambang, Cambodia.

Leo and Eam have two children: **Amanda Dara Ath-Spence**, born October 22, 1992, and **Charles Matthew Ath-Spence**, born on September 4, 1996. Both children were born in Lincoln. Leo and Eam divorced in 2008.

JULIE EVANN GLASS   (1963 –   ; < Gene V < Edwin Orville < Edwin Origen)
GENERATION 14

Julie Evann Glass is the only child of Gene and Sharon Lea (Grossoehme) Glass, born on October 18, 1963, in Madison, Wisconsin. Julie attended elementary and secondary school in Boulder, Colorado, graduating from Fairview High School in 1982. She attended Chaminade University in Honolulu, Hawaii, for two years before transferring to the University of Colorado, from which she graduated with a BA degree in Dance in 1986.

Julie married **Piet Mark Sawvel** on May 28, 1995, in Boulder. Piet was born on November 7, 1966, in Aspen, Colorado to Dorothy and Keith Sawvel. He was raised in Aspen, Montrose, Colorado, and Appleton, Wisconsin.

Julie purchased a dance studio, Backstage Ballet and Jazz, in Longmont, Colorado, in 1988, which she operated for about 15 years before selling the business. As of 2016, the business was still operating under the name Longmont Dance Threatre. Julie began work in the Human Relations office of a security software company – LogRhythm – in Boulder in 2011; in 2015 she was promoted to Senior Human Resources Coordinator.

Glass Family in America

Julie and Piet have adopted two children: **Isaac Benjamin Sawvel**, born April 28, 1997, in Boulder, and **Eliana Rose Sawvel**, born May 22, 2001.

AIMEE KATHLEEN GLASS
(1974 –   ; < Paul < Milton Collins < Edwin Origen)
GENERATION 14

Aimee Kathleen (Glass) Richards married Darren Scott Richards. They have five sons: Jarred Michael, Jaden Christopher, Ethan James, Matthew Joel, and Shane Joseph. Aimee and Darren are divorced.

ANNE MARIE GLASS
(1976 –   ; < Paul < Milton Collins < Edwin Origen)
GENERATION 14

Anne Marie Glass is the second daughter or Paul and Terri Glass. She was born on July 1, 1976, in Fontana, California. Anne attended schools and college in California: Calimesa Elementary; Yucaipa Middle school; Yucaipa High School. She graduated from Yucca Valley Christian School and attended Crafton Hills College in Yucaipa, California. Anne married Roland Douglas Hoover in 1999. The couple lived in Yucaipa in 2016.

Anne and Roland have two sons: Bryan Roland Hoover born in Pontiac, Michigan, in 2003, and Trevor David Hoover born in Redlands, California in 2003.

Anne worked at the Forest Home Christian Conference Center throughout high school, and in the early 2000s was a barista at Starbucks Coffee in Michigan until Bryan was born.

SCOTT CHANDLER GLASS
(1985 – ; < Glenn Russell < Milton Collins < Edwin Origen)
GENERATION 14

Scott Chandler Glass is the son of Glenn Russell Glass and Shelley Belinda Glass. He was born in 1985 and adopted soon after birth. He was raised during his adolescent years in Lake Havasu, Arizona. Between 2010 and 2013, he was employed as a Nursing Assistant in the Phoenix, Arizona area.

KAYLIN NICOLE (GLASS) CORNELISON
(1993 – ; < Clint Lyle < Lyle Calvin < Edwin Origen)
GENERATION 14

Kaylin Nicole Glass was born March 3, 1993, in Ocala, Florida, to Clint Lyle Glass and Karen Boehmer. She graduated from Forest High School in Ocala, Florida. In 2011, Kaylin was attending Indian River State College in Fort Pierce, Florida, where she participated in Women's Volleyball. Kaylin married **Eric Corn Cornelison**, also of Ocala, on August 23, 2015. In 2016, she and Eric were residing in Pooler, Georgia, where Eric is stationed with the U.S. Army. In 2016, Eric was transferred to Fort Carson in Colorado Springs, Colorado.

COLTON JOSHUA GLASS
(2007 –   ; Clint Lyle < Lyle Calvin < Edwin Origen)
GENERATION 14

Colton Joshua Glass was born May 31, 2007, in Ocala, Florida, to Clint Lyle Glass and Karen Boehmer Glass. Colton entered the 4th grade in the Ocala, Florida, public schools in August, 2016.

JASON SCOTT GLASS
(1978 –   ; < Gregory Scott < Edwin Gordon < Edwin Orville)
GENERATION 15

Jason Scott Glass, born on December 4, 1978, in Denver, Colorado, is the elder son of Gregory Scott Glass and Linda S. Buchholtz. He attended Columbine Elementary School in Denver, Ken Caryl Middle School in Littleton, Colorado, and graduated from Columbine High School in May, 1997. Jason earned a Bachelor of Science degree in Finance from Colorado State University in Fort Collins, Colorado, in December, 2001. He completed an MBA at Regis University, Denver, in December 2011.

Jason married Heather Elizabeth Sherman (see BRIEF BIOGRAPHIES) on July 25, 2009, in Cozumel, Mexico.

Jason was employed from 2012 to 2015 by Epicor Software as a Senior Manager for Channel Sales. In 2014, Jason and his family took up residence in Boston, thus completing a circle that began almost 400 years earlier with the immigration of the four Glass siblings to Boston from Somerset, England in 1637. In 2016, Jason, Heather, and son **Jackson Paul** returned to Denver and took up residence at 901 Harrison Street. Daughter Cameron Elizabeth was born in Denver on April 12, 2016.

JOSHUA STEVEN GLASS
(1981 –   ; < Gregory Scott < Edwin Gordon < Edwin Orville)
GENERATION 15

Joshua Steven Glass, born on November 7, 1981, in Denver, Colorado, is the younger son of Gregory Scott Glass and Linda S. Buchholtz. Josh attended Columbine Hills Elementary School, Ken Caryl Middle School, and Columbine High School, where he graduated in 2000. Columbine High School in Jefferson County, Colorado, was the site of one of the largest mass murders in U.S. history. Two students, who shall remain unnamed, entered the school at

11:19 a.m. on April 20, 1999. They were armed with two shotguns, two 9 mm hand guns, a fire bomb to divert firefighters, propane tanks converted to bombs placed in the cafeteria, 99 explosive devices, and bombs rigged in cars. The pair murdered 12 students, a teacher, and then committed suicide. Twenty-one students survived their injuries. Josh was working out in the gymnasium during the massacre. Had the assailants turned right into the gym instead of left into the cafeteria, he might not have survived.

After high school, Josh attended Colorado State University in Fort Collins and Front Range Community College. He was awarded an Associates degree in Automobile Technology and has found employment in that field since. In 2015, he was employed by Advance Auto, and automobile parts retail company. His goal is to own his own home, where he can restore old cars.

Josh is in a relationship with Sarah McGill. They reside on South Dudley Street in Denver.

At an unusually young age, Josh developed Chronic Myelogenous Leukemia, and has actively and successfully participated in its treatment for several years preceding 2016, when this account was written.

AMANDA LYNN RYD
(1990 –   ; Karen Sue < Edwin Gordon < Edwin Orville)
GENERATION 15

Amanda ("Mandie") Lynn Ryd was born on September 16, 1990, at 9:16 a.m. at St. Anthony Hospital in Denver, Colorado. She was adopted at an early age by Karen (Glass) and Jan Ryd. Her adoption was finalized October 28, 1991, a year and a day before her brother Erik was born. Mandie attended Hutchinson Elementary School (1995-2002), Dunstan Middle School (2002-2005), and she graduated from Green Mountain

High School in May 2009. Mandie attended the University of Colorado Boulder (2009 -2010), Red Rocks Community College (2011- 2013), and she graduated from Metropolitan State University of Denver in 2016 with a Bachelor of Arts and a minor in secondary education. Mandie has excelled in school at all levels. Her career plans focus on public school teaching.

Mandie describes her interests and hobbies in her own words: "I love animals and being outside. In my free time, I enjoy hikes with my dog, an Australian Shepard named Pepper. I have always loved to ride horses and have been riding since I was 8 years old. I love to read, draw, and do any type of craft. Growing up, I enjoyed playing basketball, bike riding, horseback riding, Girl Scout activities."

ERIK SABIN RYD
(1993 –   ; Karen Sue < Edwin Gordon < Edwin Orville)
GENERATION 15

Erik Ryd was born on August 29, 1993, in Conifer, Colorado. He attended schools in Lakewood, Colorado, and graduated in 2011 from Colorado Connections Academy. He was employed as a manager in his parents' chain of automobile repair businesses. In 2016, he was working at a Lee Myles automobile repair business as office manager in Boulder, Colorado.

AXEL GORDON RYD
(1997 –   ; Karen Sue < Edwin Gordon < Edwin Orville)
GENERATION 15

Axel Ryd was born on August 26, 1997, in Lakewood, Colorado where he attended elementary and secondary school. He graduated from Green Mountain High School in 2015, and entered Fort Lewis College in Durango, Colorado.

Glass Family in America

KYLE LEE GLASS
(1986 –   ; < Zachary Alan < Edwin Gordon < Edwin Orville)
GENERATION 15

Kyle Glass is the son of **Zachary Alan Glass** (pictured with **Dane Alan Glass**) and Sandra (Hughes) Glass. Kyle is one of a twin pair (with Dane Alan Glass) born on August 8, 1986, in Denver, Colorado. Kyle and Dane were born in the 24th week of their mother's pregnancy and weighed 1 lb. 12 oz. each. For many years, they were the smallest surviving twins ever born in Denver. Kyle suffered hypoxia during delivery and has struggled with epilepsy and associated brain injuries for 30 years. He lives with his parents in Elizabeth, Colorado.

DANE ALAN GLASS
(1986 –   ; < Zachary Alan < Edwin Gordon < Edwin Orville)
GENERATION 15

Dane Glass is the twin brother of Kyle Glass (see above). Dane did not suffer from complications during delivery to the same extent as his brother. Nevertheless, both Dane and Kyle spent the first 4 or 5 months of their lives hospitalized.

Dane attended school in Elizabeth, Colorado, and graduated from Elizabeth High School. He took further education at a technical school in Aurora, Colorado, and in 2016 was employed in the field of small engine repair in Castle Rock, Colorado.

AMANDA DARA ATH-SPENCE
(1992 –   ; < Leonard Dean < Ellen Gay <Edwin Orville)
GENERATION 15

Amanda was born on October 22, 1992, in Lincoln at Bryan LGH East hospital. She attended schools at Roper Elementary, Park Middle School, and Lincoln High School. She graduated from Lincoln High School in 2010. She attended Kaplan University and earned an Associate Degree in Medical Technology. She was employed at Lancaster Manor and for the Department of Homeland Security. Amanda and Christopher William Joseph Greggs were a couple starting about 2007, and they have two children: Caydin Warren Greggs, born October 26, 2010, and Maleah Rene Greggs, born December 12, 2014. In 2016, they were not living together.

CHARLES MATTHEW ATH-SPENCE
(1996 –   ; < Leonard Dean < Ellen Gay < Edwin Orville)
GENERATION 15

Charlie was born on September 4, 1996, in Lincoln, at Bryan LGH East hospital. Charlie attended Roper Elementary School, Culler Middle School, and Lincoln Northeast High School. He graduated in May 2014, having consistently made the Honor Role in middle and high school.

The John Dorn family sponsored the immigration of the Ath family from Cambodia to Minneapolis in 1984.

Glass Family in America

ISAAC BENJAMIN SAWVEL
(1997 –   ; < Julie Evann < Gene V < Edwin Orville)
GENERATION 15

Isaac Benjamin Sawvel was born on April 28, 1997, at Boulder Community Hospital in Boulder, Colorado. Within 24 hours, he was given to the care of his adoptive parents, Julie Evann Glass (Generation 14) and Piet Mark Sawvel. Isaac attended Eagle Crest Elementary School, Altona Middle School, and Silver Creek High School, all in Longmont, Colorado. He graduated from Silver Creek in 2015, and enrolled in Front Range Community College that fall. In high school, he participated on the high school tennis team as a doubles specialist. In 2013, after placing 2nd in the regional finals, Isaac and his partner were 2 of 5 team members who represented Silver Creek at the state tennis tournament finals in Pueblo. In 2016, he enrolled in Northeastern Community College in Sterling, Colorado.

ELIANA ROSE SAWVEL
(2001 –   ; < Julie Evann < Gene V < Edwin Orville)
GENERATION 15

Eliana Rose Sawvel was born on May 22, 2001. Throughout the first four or five months of her life, she was in the care of her birth mother, then later, a foster mother. In the fall of 2001, she was placed in the care of her adoptive parents, Julie Evann Glass and Piet Mark Sawvel. She attended Eagle Crest Elementary School, Altona Middle School, and in the fall of 2015 entered Silver Creek High School, all in Longmont, Colorado. She is an accomplished equestrian; and in June

2015, she participated in the national finals of the Interscholastic High School Equestrian Association in Oklahoma City. She served as a cheerleader for her high school for the 2016-2017 school year.

JARRED MICHAEL RICHARDS
(1999 –   ; < Aimee Kathleen < Paul < Milton Collins)
GENERATION 15
Jarred Michael was born to Aimee Kathleen Glass and Darren Scott Richards on July 17, 1999.

JADEN CHISTOPHER RICHARDS
(2001 –   ; < Aimee Kathleen < Paul < Milton Collins)
GENERATION 15
Jaden Christopher was born to Aimee Kathleen Glass and Darren Scott Richards on July 29, 2001.

ETHAN JAMES RICHARDS
(2004 –   ; < Aimee Kathleen < Paul < Milton Collins)
GENERATION 15
Ethan James was born to Aimee Kathleen Glass and Darren Scott Richards on January 29, 2004.

MATTHEW JOEL RICHARDS
(2007 –   ; < Aimee Kathleen < Paul < Milton Collins)
GENERATION 15
Matthew Joel was born to Aimee Kathleen Glass and Darren Scott Richards on November 6, 2007.

SHANE JOSEPH RICHARDS
(2009 –   ; < Aimee Kathleen < Paul < Milton Collins)
GENERATION 15
Shane Joseph was born to Aimee Kathleen Glass and Darren Scott Richards on October 13, 2009.

Glass Family in America

L to R: Ethan James Richards, Aimee Glass-Richards, Mathew Joel Richards, Bryan Roland Hoover, Teri Glass. Anne Marie Glass-Hoover, Trevor David Hoover, Jarred Michael Hoover, Shane Joseph Hoover

BRYAN ROLAND HOOVER
(2003 –   ; < Anne Marie < Paul < Milton Collins)
GENERATION 15

Bryan is the older son of Anne Marie Glass and Roland Douglas Hoover, born in Pontiac, Michigan, on January 16, 2003. Bryan, a 15th

generation descendant of John Glasse of Somerset, England, was born just 15 miles north of Nankin, Michigan, where Edwin Zenis Glass, a 10th generation descendant and Bryan's 4 times great-grandfather, was born in 1857, nearly 150 years earlier.

TREVOR DAVID HOOVER
(2007 –   ; < Anne Marie < Paul < Milton Collins)
GENERATION 15

Trevor is the younger son of Anne Marie Glass and Roland Douglas Hoover, born in Redlands, California, on January 31, 2007.

CAYDIN WARREN GREGGS
(2010 – ; < Amanda < Leonard Dean < Ellen Gay)
GENERATION 16

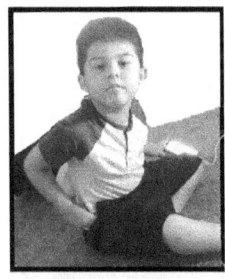
Caydin was born to Amanda Ath-Spence and Christopher Greggs on October 26, 2010, at St. Elizabeth's hospital in Lincoln, Nebraska. Caydin was their first child.

MALEAH RENE GREGGS
(2014 – ; < Amanda < Leonard Dean < Ellen Gay)
GENERATION 16

Maleah was born to Amanda Ath-Spence and Christopher Greggs on December 12, 2014, at St. Elizabeth's hospital in Lincoln, Nebraska. Maleah was their second child.

JACKSON PAUL GLASS
(2013 – ; < Jason Scott < Gregory Scott < Edwin Gordon)
GENERATION 16

Jackson Paul Glass was born to Heather Elizabeth Sherman and Jason Scott Glass on June 26, 2013, at Rose Medical Center, Denver, Colorado. His first two years were spent in Boston, Massachusetts, thus completing a circle that began with Henry Glass's immigration from Somerset, England, to Boston in 1637. In 2016, he resided in Denver.

CAMERON ELIZABETH GLASS
(2016 – ; < Jason Scott < Gregory Scott < Edwin Gordon)
GENERATION 16

Cameron Elizabeth Glass, sister of Jackson Paul Glass, was born to Heather Elizabeth Sherman and Jason Scott Glass at 8:20 p.m. on April 12, 2016, at Rose Medical Center, Denver, Colorado. She weighed 7 lbs 10 oz. Her parents had recently returned to Denver to make their home after having lived two years in Boston in connection with Heather's work.

BRIEF BIOGRAPHIES

ATH, EAM (1966 –   ; < Ath Bhy)

Eam Ath, wife of Leonard Dean Spence, is the daughter of Ath Bhy and Leoup Sor. She was born April 13, 1966, in Battambang, Cambodia. Eam Ath (known as Amy upon receiving her United States citizenship) arrived in the Minneapolis area with her mother's family in 1984. There was a mix-up of names when the family arrived in the United States; she was given her sister's name, Eam. Ath Bhy, father, died of dysentery in Battambang. Leoup was left with four children, under the age of ten years of age, to seek refuge in Thailand. The eldest son was enscripted by the Khmer Rouge at age fourteen. The families reconnected in the mid 1990s.

Eam married Leonard Dean Spence in Lincoln, Nebraska, on April 5, 1997. Leo and Eam have two children: Amanda Dara Ath-Spence, born October 22, 1992, and Charles Matthew Ath-Spence, born on September 4, 1996. Both children were born in Lincoln, Nebraska. Leo and Eam divorced in 2008.

BAERENBACH, HELEN VIRGINIA (1922 – 2016)

Helen Baerenbach was born in 1922 in the borough of Manhattan, New York, New York. She was born to Michael Paul Baerenbach Jr. and Julia Margaret Nehr. Michael was a marine machinist working for the Bethlehem Steel Company in Hoboken, New Jersey.

Helen married Gayland Warren Glass on June 24, 1943, in Manhattan. The couple lived in Manhattan in the mid-1940s,

Lincoln, Nebraska, in the 1950s, Grand Island, Nebraska in the 1960s, and Lakewood, Colorado, thereafter. Helen died on July 5, 2016, at an assisted living facility in Parker, Colorado.

Helen's mother, Julia, was born to Jakob Nehr and Magdealena (Lena) Wolfer in 1900. According to family stories, Jakob Nehr was a great cook who opened his first restaurant in 1891 at 83 Allen Street in lower Manhattan. Jakob and Lena Nehr worked hard and did very well in the restaurant business. By 1898, they had earned enough to retire and buy a four-story apartment building on the East River at **436 E. 59th Street** in upscale Sutton Place. Many Nehrs and their families, including Helen, lived in this building over a period of more than 30 years.

BOEHMER, KAREN (1966 –   )

Karen Boehmer was born January 14, 1966. Karen married Clint Lyle Glass on October 14, 1989, in Ocala, Florida. Their daughter Kaylin was born March 3, 1993, in Ocala; their son, Colton Joshua Glass, was born on May 31, 2007. In 2016, Karen and Clint were members of the Greenway Elementary School Parent Teacher Organization, for which Karen served as President.

BUCHHOLTZ, LINDA S. (1957 –   )

Linda Buchholtz was the first wife of Gregory Scott Glass. She was born June 30, 1957, in Superior, Wisconsin. She and Greg were married on May 13, 1978, in Denver,

Colorado. Their union produced two sons: Jason Scott Glass, born on December 4, 1978, and Joshua Steven Glass, born on November 7, 1981. They divorced in September, 2000. Linda's married name is Linda Bourgeois, and in 2016 she worked as a realtor in Denver, Colorado.

COGAN, MARY (1595 – 1631)

Mary Cogan was born on November 22, 1595, in Taunton, Somerset, England, to Henry Cogan and Joan Boridge. She married James Glass(e) on January 24, 1613. She is the mother of the four Glass siblings who immigrated at Massachusetts in 1637. Two other children, Richard and Mary, probably remained in England; Richard died at age 13. Henry Glass was an indentured servant of Mary's brother, Henry, who emigrated with the siblings. The Cogan line reaches back centuries in southwestern England and Wales. Robert Shaver, the author of *From Great Britain To Western Illinois: A Glass-Cone-Smith Genealogical Sequel*, has traced a bit of the history of the Cogan family. Shaver's text is quoted here:

> The Cogan family has been well researched by George E. McCracken in a series of articles entitled "Early Cogans English and American" (1956-1957, New England Historical and Genealogical Register, v. 110). The article in volume 111, pages 168-187, is especially interesting to us because it deals in more detail than I did herein for the Glasses and Cogans of Taunton, England, and even tells of their earliest history in New England.
>
> More than that, these articles reveal that the Cogans were widespread in the southwestern English counties, some leaving enviable records. Further, the first article traces the origin of the name as far back as 1182 to a Miles de

Cogan, one of the Norman conquerors of Ireland. The Normans also conquered much of Wales at about the same time, approximately 100 years after they began their conquest of England in 1066. Although absolute proof is lacking, McCracken believed that most of the Cogans descended from a baronial family that took its name from a fief (land held from a lord in the feudal system) in Glamorganshire, the southernmost county in Wales. In early modern times the remnants of this fief consisted of the small hamlet of Cogan a few miles south of Cardiff.

As for the Taunton Cogans, their ties with other and older Cogan generations are scarcely verified. But a Henry Cogan married an Elizabeth Carye at Chedzoy on 1 July 1565 (McCracken, 1957, p. 168-169). These two probably were the parents of the Henry Cogan who married Joan Boridge on 30 November 1590 and who is noted ... as our oldest fairly well proved Cogan ancestor. This Henry is said to have been a clothier in Taunton. Much more research, possibly proving to be fruitless, would be needed to prove our exact Cogan lineage in the early centuries of the Norman Conquest. (Shaver, 1993, p. 161)

The Glass line could possibly be as much Welsh as it is English, considering its conjoining with the Cogan line in the 1600s.

DAVIS, GLADYS ANNETTE (1919 – 1973)

Gladys Annette Davis from Burchard, Nebraska, married Victor Buren Glass on October 13, 1947. Gladys was born on March 5, 1919, in Eckley, Yuma County, Colorado, the daughter of Milton Forest Davis and Emma Rebecca Johnston. Gladys was working as a domestic housekeeper in Vesta, Nebraska, in the household of a Lovitt family in the 1940 Census. Vic and Gladys had two children: Gary Dean and Virginia Ann. The family lived in La Puente, California, for many years. Gladys's father died in La Puente on December 7, 1963. Gladys died in Covina, California, in July 14, 1973.

DAVIS, BLANCHE (1909 – 1992)

Blanche Davis was born on May 24, 1909. She married Lyle Calvin Glass in Lincoln, Nebraska, in about 1930; they adopted a son named Clint Lyle Glass. Blanche died on August, 1, 1992, in Ocklawaha, Florida.

ELDRIDGE, THERESE PAULINE (1952 –   )

Terri is married to Paul Raymond Glass. She was born at Edwards AFB, California, on May 4, 1952, to Donald Edward Eldridge and Charlotte Viviane Eldridge. Her father was English and her mother was French. Teri received a graduate degree from Biola University in 1980. She was employed as Senior Director of Human Resources for Forest Home, Inc., Forest Falls, California, where she retired in 2003 after 17 years of service. Terri and Paul have two daughters: Aimee Kathleen and Anne Marie. They have seven grandsons: Jarred Michael Richards, Jaden Christopher Richards, Ethan James Richards, Matthew Joel Richards, Shane Joseph Richards, Bryan Roland Hoover, and Trevor David Hoover.

FULLER, HULDAH (1762 – 1813)

Huldah was the wife of Rufus Glass. Hulda Fuller was born January 26, 1762, in East Haddam, Connecticut. Huldah's father was William Fuller; her mother was Rebecca Spencer. Huldah Fuller is the Sixth Generation (3rd Great Grandchild) of Edward Fuller (died 1621 in Plymouth, Massachusetts) – who came to America on the Mayflower. Huldah was the aunt of Oliver Cowdry. Oliver was born to Huldah's sister Rebecca. Cowdry was an associate of Joseph Smith's. He acted as a scribe in writing down the first Book of Mormon, and he was the first person baptized, by Smith, as a Mormon.

FERRIS, SARAH (GLASS, PERRIN, STEPHENSON) (1821 – 1923)

Sarah was born on August 22, 1821, and died in Lincoln, Nebraska, on February 24, 1923, having lived nearly 102 years. She is buried in Wyuka Cemetery in Lincoln.

Sarah was born in Elizabethtown, New York. Her father, Eli Ferris, is a descendant in the long line of Ferrises that includes Jeffrey Ferris who migrated to Connecticut from England in the mid-1600s and was a founder of the city of Greenwich. Sarah's ancestry reaches back to Sir Richard de Wilburgham, who was born in about 1174, very likely in Shipbrook, Davenham, Cheshire, England. Sir Richard was sheriff of Chesire during the reign of Henry III. You, dear reader, may share an infinitesimally small number of genes with Sir Richard.

As a young woman of 14 years or so, Sarah left her father's family on the west shore of Lake Champlain on account of conflicts with her stepmother. She traveled west with her married sister, moving along the recently completed Erie Canal, until she reached Lake Erie, from which she traveled by boat to Detroit. The journey took three weeks and she arrived on July 4, 1836.

In the village of Nankin, only a few miles from the center of modern-day Detroit, she met and married Zenas Glass. She bore him several children before he died in 1857. Shortly after his death, Sarah married Isaac Perrin who owned a mill in nearby Perrinsville. Isaac lived only a few years after their marriage, leaving Sarah a widow for the second time. After the Civil War, she married her third husband, James H. Stephenson, on August 23, 1869. James Stephenson was born in New York on October 15, 1814. He farmed in Nankin throughout his adult life; his wealth was probably slightly above average for the region. He died on October 27, 1904, in Michigan. In the meantime, Sarah's son

Edwin Zenis had traveled west to Nebraska where he was employed as an engineer on the railroad. In about 1905, Edwin Zenis traveled back to Michigan to bring his mother to Lincoln where she spent the rest of her life.

At one point in the early part of the 20th Century, Sarah wrote the following letter to one of her grandchildren, Milton Frost, the son of Sarah's daughter, also named Sarah, and Origen Frost.

> To my dear grandson Milton Frost
>
> I have thought for long time [I] would write you in regard to what I said to you it being your mother's and my daughter thinking you did not understand   [I]t is why I am writing this so may not be any misunderstanding after I am gone.
>
> [W]ill begin at the beginning of the correspondence between your father & myself for 3 years after Ellen and Edwin left home father [circa 1876] kept saying you better sell the land[.] I would say don't want to sell it after a while he said Dickerson would buy and pay a good price. So Dickerson came said would give fifteen hundred and no more[.] I said did not want to sell it was so easy money to get away   I wrote your father asked his advice he said he thought it a very good price & if I sold it let him have the money to put in his bank. [H]e thought it a very good price so sold   let your father have seven hundred & twenty four dollars[.] [W]here would I be if had let him have all that I ever got of the 700 & 24 dollars was fifteen dollars[.] [W]hen your mother and Ruben came in April staid quite a while & the same time your father wrote to know if he could have the money another year as was

about to buy out store of goods in York   thought he could make good on the trade[.]

[A]t the same time the bank had failed and I did not know it & your mother did not tell me either. She has since told me she could not tell me about it at that time but I heard the bank had failed[.] [C]annot tell for the life of me whether it was Doe or who it was[.] [S]uppose it was your father tho it was so unrespectful I was so dazed or something   it all went from me[.] [T]his is the truth in all I write[.] [Y]our father gave me a note for the money dated Aug. 20, 1876 interest to be added to the principal at 5 per ct 26 dollars more would been ½ I was worth. I want Ed to have what is left after I am gone there will not be much after funeral expenses are paid[.] [I] think I should have the say about this if anybody.

[N]ow put yourself in my place suffering[.] [Y]ou let a party have money & they lost it by some means   would you think it right for the same party to claim a share of the other ½[?] [N]o indeed you would not nor any one else would either if they looked at it unbiased by any interest & I don't think your mother intends to either[.]

[N]ow Sape is as much my child as Ed & I love them both but do not think she should have only a reasonable price for the grave to lay me in. Ed & Eva has given me a home ever since came to Neb & will as long as I need one I expect & they ought to have what is left after I am gone. If your mother had had a home of her own I probably would have staid with her part of the time if she had wanted me too but as she had not[.] [H]ere I am & expect to be until the good Lord calls for me & hope to be ready when called[.]

[M]ay all be settled pleasantly & live friendly together is the wish & desire of your Grandmother[.] [M]ay we all be saved in that blessed land where there is no sin or sorrow is the prayer of your Grandmother[.]
                        Sarah J Stephenson

Ed is to have all after I am gone only what is spoken of within[.]

The amount of $750 in 1876 would be the rough equivalent of $16,000 in 2016.

The following letter was written by Sarah to an unknown recipient on August 14, 1911.

Sarah [her daughter] & myself were one time talking about [Name undecipherable] my daughterinlaw wanting me taken back when I passed away & buried in Newburg Cemetery. I said if it would cost less money to bury me here would rather be buried here in Lincoln cemetery for always had a horror of seeing coffins taken on a train[.] [Just] bury me inexpensive and respectful is all I ask. Sape [nickname of Sarah's daughter Sarah] said there was plenty of room on their lot for me so Ed give Sape a reasonable price for the grave. This is reasonable according to the money Sape & her husband has had of my money which was 700 seven hundred and over dollars & entirely lost to me by their misfortune. They paid 4 per ct interest while the other two children paid from 6 to 5 per cent interest as receipts will show. [D]on't get a stone that is to cost much just a little slab. [W]ant Ed to have what money is left of funeral expense. He lost almost a month wages going back to Mich after me. Now this is my idea & wishes hope and pray my 2 children live friendly & happily& strive for the better world & may we meet in heaven where is no sin or sorrow. Your affectionate mother.

[A postscript] have lived in Neb over 6 years & one year would cover all the time & more away from Ed's home. Not that have more love for one child than another but right is right the world over

would rather no stone at all

S[arah] J[ane] Stephenson

FROST, ORIGEN (1841 – 1909)

Origen Frost was born in Michigan in about 1841. The Frost family goes back as far as 1660, when they were located in the state of Maine. Origen was drafted into the Union army from Ypsilanti, Michigan, in 1863. Little is known about his service. In 1873, he was working as a conductor on the Burlington & Missouri Railroad and residing in Lincoln, Nebraska. Later in life he worked as a brakeman on the Union Pacific Railway. He married Sarah Glass in Michigan in 1874. They had at least two children: Milton D. and Reuben O. They migrated to Plattsmouth, Nebraska, between the birth of their two sons. In the 1900 U.S. Census, Origen was listed as a brakeman on the Burlington railroad, living in Stromburg, Nebraska. Stromburg was a small town 30 miles northwest of Lincoln. Origen died on December 1, 1909.

GILLETT, EVELINE (1858 – 1923)

Eveline ("Eva") Gillett, daughter of Ira Gillett and Catherine Atherton was born on July 11, 1858, in Wayne County, Michigan. She was married to Edwin Zenis Glass on March 23, 1881, in Perrinsville, Michigan. She died on July 28, 1923, in Lincoln, Nebraska. She and Edwin Zenis had one child, Edwin Origen Glass.

Eva's ancestors go back in the history of New England even further than the ancestors of her husband. Eva's four-times great-grandfather was Jonathan Gillett, who was born in 1603 in Chaffcombe, Somerset, England, the same county to which the Glasse family can be traced in mid-1500s. Jonathan was married to Mary Dolbere on March 29, 1634, in St. Andrew's Church, Colyton, Devonshire, England. Jonathan immigrated at Massachusetts Bay in 1633, four years before the arrival of the four Glass siblings. He first settled in Dorchester, Massachusetts and later moved to Windsor, Connecticut, in 1638. He died in Windsor on August 23, 1677. His wife, Mary, died in Windsor on January 5, 1685. The history of the migration of Jonathan and Mary and their fellow Puritans has been documented by the Windsor Historical Society and is available on the Internet.

The Gillett line has been researched reliably back to the Reverend William Gylette who was born in 1575 in Chaffcombe, Somerset, England. Beyond this the identification of ancestors is speculative, but may reach Antoine Thomas de Gylet, who was born in 1430, probably in Bergerac, France.

GREGGS, CHRISTOPHER WILLIAM JOSEPH (1992 –)

Chris is the partner of Amanda Ath-Spence and the father of their children Caydin Warren Greggs and Maleah Rene Greggs, who are the great-grandchildren of Ellen Gay (Glass) Spence. Chris graduated from Lincoln High School and is resident in Lincoln in 2016.

GROSSOEHME, SHARON LEA (1940 –)

Sharon Grossoehme was born on May 4, 1940, in Lincoln, Nebraska, to William Grossoehme and Nannie M. Dickerson. William was born on March 30, 1895. It was said that Will was born on an island in the Missouri River: probably a portion of land surrounded at times by a changing river channel. He died on February 11, 1972, in Lincoln, Nebraska, from complications arising from prostate cancer. The Grossoehme family were immigrants from Germany in the mid- to late-1800s. William's parents (Ernst Furchtegott Grossoehme – born June 8, 1853 – and Anna Amalie Therese Turke) settled in the southeastern tip of the state of Nebraska. Nannie M. Dickerson was born to James Hiram Dickerson and Mahala Elizabeth Mabry in 1900 in Brock, Nebraska. Mahala's line can be traced to John Gilliam (Guillim) who was born in England in 1565 and died in 1621.

William ("Will") was a biology teacher at Lincoln Northeast High School, and Nan was a homemaker. Sharon attended elementary school at Huntington Elementary in University Place, and junior and senior high school at Northeast Junior and Senior High School, where she was consistently on the Honor Role, and held several sought-after positions: Editor of the student newspaper, cheerleader, Sports Banquet Attendant, Sophomore May Day Attendant, and Senior May Day Queen. She was an accomplished pianist. She married Gene V Glass on August 16, 1959, at St. Paul Methodist Church in University Place, Lincoln. Their daughter Julie Evann was born October 18, 1963, in Madison, Wisconsin. Sharon and Gene were divorced in 1975. She held various jobs in her adult life, including dental assistant, medical assistant, and secretary – the latter position at a technology company (Storage Technology) in Louisville, Colorado.

She married Glen George Arp in Boulder, Colorado, on June 16, 1980. Glen died on June 7, 2008, in Brush, Colorado. Sharon married Paul Baker in Brush in November, 2013. In 2016, she was resident in Brush, Colorado.

HOOVER, ROLAND DOUGLAS (1976 –   )

Roland Hoover is married to Anne Marie Glass, the daughter of Paul Glass. Roland was born in San Bernardino, California, on February 10, 1976. He grew up in Yucaipa, California. He met Anne in junior high school and started dating her in his senior year of high school. Roland and Anne were married after he graduated from Cal Poly Pomona Tech with a Bachelors degree in Mechanical Engineering Science. Roland and Anne Marie have two sons: Bryan and Trevor.

HILLIARD, ELEANOR IDAMAE (1920 – 2010)

Idamae Hilliard married **Milton Collins Glass** in Lincoln, Nebraska. She was born in Lincoln, Nebraska, on June 12, 1920.

Idamae's parents were Ralph Gerard Hilliard and Mary May Pelmulder, both of whom were born in Iowa in the 1890s. Ida's ancestors can be traced back to William Hilliard who resided in Duxbury, Plymouth County, Massachusetts, in the 1640s. Descendants of the Glass siblings (James, Roger, Henry, and Amy) also lived in Duxbury at that same time. The furthest back that the Hilliard line has been traced for this account is the birth of a William Hilliard in 1614 in England.

After Milton's death, Idamae met **Clyde Grafton Baldosser**. Clyde was slightly older than Idamae. They became friends; eventually they started dating and finally he talked her into marrying him. Clyde was the only son of a wealthy San Gabriel Valley landowner, Frank P. Baldosser.

Sometime around the late 1880s, Clyde's father Frank left his home state of Ohio and went West. He found gold in California oranges. Quite quickly, he purchased land and then more land; he put in groves and strawberry fields. Frank needed hands to work in his fields. Needing help, Frank sent recruitment letters to Ohio. Among them were two letters to a Miss Emma Grafton. The first letter was to ask her to come pick the coming harvest because he knows she is a hard worker. The second was to tell her that the hay had turned out fine and made more than four hundred tons. The letter goes on to say: "If you are coming back to California and want to work I will give you eighteen dollars for your time, fifteen after the plowing is over and during the harvest season I will give you twenty per month. ... Let me hear from you soon."

Miss Emma Grafton loaded up everything she had as a result of this second letter and rode west in a covered wagon. She worked the packing houses and lived in the women's dorms. She must have kept company with Frank because they married the following year. Meanwhile, Frank and his cronies established a local, and consistent, source of water for themselves in the local San Gabriel mountains. A dam was built, water channels built and the Azusa Valley Water District was established. Frank, his son Clyde, and by a wild coincidence the brother of Paul's future wife Teri Eldridge, held board positions on that small, but significant, water company. It was the last water district in the Los Angeles Metropolitan Water District area to incorporate into the larger holding. Clyde was the sole inheritor of his parents' land holdings and accumulated significant wealth. Clyde and Idamae owned the Resort at

Silver Lake on the June Lake Loop near Mammoth, California. In retirement Idamae and Clyde traveled around the world. They settled in Yucaipa, CA.

Clyde died on July 12, 1995 in Yucaipa, San Bernardino, California. She died on March 23, 2010, in Yucaipa, California.

HUGHES, SANDRA LEE (1957 –   )

Sandy was born September 28, 1957 in Cleveland, Ohio. She married Zachary Alan Glass in 1985 in Denver. Sandy and Zach have two sons, Kyle and Dane.

JONES, NORA ELLEN (1888 – 1968)

Nora Ellen Jones was born on September 20, 1888, at Imperial, Nebraska, which is 28 miles southeast of Grant, Nebraska. Ellen was the daughter of Wilson Ballard Avery Jones and Emma Boardman Bragg. Ella was the wife of Edwin Origen Glass. They were married on November 25, 1908 in Grant, Perkins, Nebraska. She is descended on her mother's side (Emma Boardman Bragg) from Captain Christopher Newport.

It's unclear when the Jones family came to western Nebraska, but it was probably in the early 1880s. Jones was of Welsh descent with known ancestors in Wales in the mid-1500s. Family lore maintains that he was alcoholic and abandoned the family at some point long after migrating to Nebraska.[26] Ellen maintained a life-long aversion to alcohol. Wilson

---

[26] There is likely some truth to this family fable. By 1910, Wilson no longer appears in the same household as Emma. The 1920 US Census shows "Ballard Jones," age 66 living as a boarder in West Virginia; his occupation is listed as "peddler." His marital status is listed as "Divorced." Emma Jones appears in the 1925 Kansas Census living with her son Samuel in Kansas.

Ballard Avery Jones died on Christmas Eve, 1926, in Medway, Hamilton County, Kansas, and was buried in Syracuse, Kansas. Through Wilson's mother, Elizabeth Ann Miller and her father, Brice Miller, the line can be traced back to James Wolfe, the hero of the Battle of the Plains of Abraham[27]. The Bragg line is also quite well known and likewise can be traced to Virginia and to the early settlement of the colony.

Ellen recalled being fearful as a child due to the wars between the Sioux tribe and the U.S. military in western Nebraska, even though the hostilities ended in 1890. Ellen died in Lincoln, Nebraska, in 1968, from complications of Parkinson's disease.

LINTT, GRACE VIRGINIA (1912 – 1986)

Grace Virginia Lintt was born in Lincoln, Nebraska, on February 16, 1912, to Gordon Price Lintt and Emma Mills. Grace's family lived at 4220 Lenox Street in Lincoln. Grace Lintt married Edwin Orville Glass on December 19, 1929, in Lincoln, Nebraska.

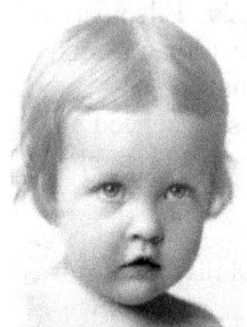

The Lintt family, though having claimed to be English, were in fact descended from Germans who entered the U.S. through Philadelphia in the mid-1700s. Conrath Thomas Lind arrived in Philadelphia in 1752 from Germany aboard a ship called The Snow Ketty. The Lind ancestors – later to be Lintts – farmed in Pennsylvania for a few generations. Just as the Glass family in New England during the Revolutionary War found it to their advantage – and perhaps, safety – to create the myth of Scottish ancestry, so too was it to the advantage of the Lintts to disguise their German ancestry during WWI in Nebraska. (The family name Lintt was actually a construction of a teacher of Grace's father, Gordon Price Lintt,

---

[27] Major General James Wolfe was a British officer, known for his training reforms but remembered chiefly for his victory over the French battle at the Battle of the Plains of Abraham in Canada in 1759. The battle secured Canada for the British.

when he was in elementary school and was being teased about having a name that sounded like "lint." The name of the new arrivals in the U.S. was Lind; German pronunciation gives the final "d" a hard sound.) Grace Lintt's father, Gordon, was employed by the newspaper as the foreman of the pressroom. It may have been through this connection that Orville Glass met Grace Virginia Lintt.

Grace died on May 10, 1986, at the age of 74 from what was probably Alzheimer's disease. Her descent was excruciatingly slow, having taken more than 10 years.

MARTINEZ, SUSAN (1953 –   )

Susan Martinez married Gregory Scott Glass (Generation 15) on October 12, 2001, in Honolulu, Hawaii.

Susan gives this account of her long friendship with Greg that eventually led to marriage:

> Greg and I met at Euclid Junior High School, Littleton, Colorado, in October 1968 in math class. We became instant best friends. We stayed best friends in high school and never lost touch. I married right after high school, and Greg went off to college. We exchanged Christmas cards and occasionally bumped into each other. I had three daughters, eventually divorced, and was single for thirteen years. When the tragedy at Columbine High School occurred in 1999, I knew that Greg's kids had to be attending that school so I tracked him down to inquire about Josh. He returned my call days later and we caught up on all the kids, families, jobs, and the like. Some time later we ran into to each other. Greg was separated from his first wife then. We started

crying on each other's shoulders, back to being each other's sounding board like when we were kids. After some time we started going to lunch and then lunch and dinner. Yada yada yada. We were married October 12, 2001 in Honolulu.

Susan was born November 28, 1953, in Denver, Colorado. Susan's parents are **Apolonio ("Paul") Martinez** and **Mabel Margarite Marquez**. Paul Martinez was born on May 10, 1926, in Dawson, New Mexico. Today, Dawson is a ghost town 15 miles southwest of Raton. Mabel Marquez was born on January 20, 1926, in Denver, Colorado. Paul and Mabel had a daughter in addition to Susan. Mary Ann was born on November 13, 1958, in Denver.

Susan graduated from Arapahoe High School, Littleton, Colorado, in 1972. She married Frank Albert Hanneman on March 24, 1973, in Littleton. Susan and Frank had three daughters: Connie Sue (Hanneman) Steele, born on September 18, 1975; Christy Lynn (Hanneman) Haas, born on November 15, 1976; and Cindy (Hanneman) Butman, born on January 29, 1979. All three daughters were born at Swedish Hospital in Englewood, Colorado. Susan and Frank divorced in December, 1988.

Susan had a long work history beginning immediately after high school. From 1972 to 1974, she was employed by Diners Club International. She was a bill collector for J.C. Penny's for two years. Some employment grew out of her daughters' activities: Office Mgr. and Costume designer for almost 20 years at Ballet Arts Center, and coaching elite gymnasts. For several years, Susan was employed by Continental Airlines in a variety of positions, culminating in playing a support role to employees and dealing with special problems from tragedies to customer misbehavior. For several years prior to 2016,

Glass Family in America

Susan has been active in politics, playing a prominent role in the Jefferson County Democratic Party.

Susan and Greg have nine grandchildren/step-grandchildren. From Susan's daughter Connie: Michel Alexander Steele (born 11/29/1998); Francessca Marie Steele (born 1/30/2001); Izabella Antoenette Steele (born 4/19/2002); and Dominica Lee Steele (born 7/14/2003). Susan's daughter Christy has two children: Thomas Brian Haas (born 11/11/2004), and Abbey Rose Haas (born 10/26/2007). Cindy's daughter is Madeline Monroe Butman (born 1/10/2008). Greg's grandchildren are the son and daughter of his son Jason: Jackson Paul Glass (born 6/26/2013) and Cameron Elizabeth Glass (born 4/12/2016).

Susan's ancestors on both sides were Spanish and long established in the New World, having been traced back to Spain around the time of Christopher Columbus. Juan Montes Vigil, ancestor of the Martinez line, arrived in Mexico from Castilla, Spain, in 1611. Juan's descendants first settled in what is now New Mexico in 1692. Donaciano Vigil was appointed the second governor of the territory of New Mexico in 1847.

Susan's father's family played a key role in the history of the State of New Mexico. Paul Martinez's grandfather was Candelario Vigil (born on February 2, 1877, in San Wapello, New Mexico). A resident of Union County, Vigil was a prominent figure on the New Mexico political scene both before and after it became a state in 1912. He attended school in Wagon Mound, New Mexico. In 1897, he married Carolina Vigil (1878-1941) with whom he had seven children. Candelario is recorded as being "*one of the most successful stockraisers*" in the Union County area, owning a large amount of American Hereford cattle.

The *Representative New Mexicans* notes that he was a notary public and served a term on the Union County Board of Education from 1902-1904.

In 1911, Candelario became a delegate to the New Mexico Constitutional Convention. This convention was of major importance in New Mexico history as it drew up the first state constitution; and within two years of its creation, New Mexico became the 47th state. In 1912, he was elected as a Republican to the New Mexico State House of Representatives. Candelario died on March 14, 1941, in Clayton, Union County, New Mexico, where he is buried. Carolina Vigil died a few months after her husband in September, 1941, and was interred alongside him in Clayton.

On Susan's mother's side, Geronimo Marquez (born in 1560) was the Maese de Campo of the troops which joined Juan de Oñate y Salazar[28] in 1600. Geronimo was a native of Sanlucar de Barrameda in southern Spain. He was described as swarthy and black-bearded. His wife and five grown sons traveled with him to Nuevo México. His name runs through all the Onate annals as an adventurous leader. As late as 1631, Geronimo and his family were living at their ranch at Acomilla, about 45 miles south of present-day Albuquerque.

Susan reports that members of the Marquez family are finding Native American and Jewish roots through DNA analysis. The latter would not be surprising since the surname Marquez is widely known as of Sephardic Jewish origin.

PONTUS, MARY ELIZABETH (1622 – 1690)

Mary was the wife of James Glass, immigrant to America in 1637 and grandson of John Glasse of Somerset, England. Mary Pontus was born on October 15, 1622, in the city of Leyden in the Netherlands. The Pilgrims left England seeking religious freedom and first migrated to the Netherlands. Eventually finding matters no better there, they returned to England and prepared for their migration to America. This accounts for Mary's birth in Leyden. Mary died on February 3, 1690, in Plymouth. Mary's mother was Wybra Hansen, a name that James and Mary later conferred on one of their daughters. Wybra was a native of the

---

[28] Juan de Oñate y Salazar was a conquistador from New Spain, explorer, and colonial governor of the Santa Fe de Nuevo México province in the Viceroyalty of New Spain.

Netherlands. Mary's father was William Pontus, who was born in Dover, Kent, England, in 1586.

After James's death, Mary was wed to Philip Delano (1602 – 1681) of Duxbury. Philip was also born in Leyden, Netherlands, and arrived in Plymouth in 1621, one year after the Mayflower, on the ship Fortune.

RATCLIFF, SHELLY BELINDA (Abt. 1955 –   )

Shelly is married to Glenn Russell Glass.

ROSENTHAL, ANDREA DIANE (SAYERS) (1977 –   )

Andrea Diane (Sayers) Rosenthal is married to Kyle Nathan Rosenthal, stepson of Gene V Glass. Andrea was born on August 23, 1977, in Phoenix, Arizona, to Kathy Sue (Eblen) Sayers and Warren Kent Sayers. Warren was born March 11, 1935; he died on May 1, 1993, and is buried at the National Memorial Cemetery of Arizona. Andrea's father was a stock trader, who was born in Denver, Colorado. He served in the U.S. Navy in the Korean War. Kathy and Warren were married for approximately eight years. Andrea has a half-sister, Kelly Elizabeth Sayers, and half-brother, Chris Sayers.

Kathy Sue Sayers, Andrea's mother, was born on March 23, 1949, in Atlantic, Iowa, to Tom and Beulah Eblen. Kathy and Andrea's father Warren lived briefly in Greenwich, Connecticut, when Andrea was an infant.

Andrea attended Village Meadows Elementary School, Deer Valley Middle School, and graduated from Barry Goldwater High School in Glendale, Arizona, in 1995. Andrea enrolled at Arizona State University in the fall of 1995. Four years later, she was awarded a Bachelor of Arts degree in Business Management. While at ASU, she was a member of the Sigma Kappa Sorority. In the fall of 1999, Andrea relocated to San Francisco, California, to live with Kyle Rosenthal. The couple resided for a few years at Fort Mason in San Francisco. Andrea's first employment in San Francisco was with the cosmetics company, Bare Escentuals. Although primarily responsible for events planning and brand awareness, she was often engaged for modeling and television marketing appearances.

Andrea and Kyle were married on April 3, 2004, in Tempe, Arizona. Andrea began employment at Pacific Gas and Electric in October, 2010, as an events planner. Andrea and Kyle's daughter Bianca Lauren Rosenthal was born on February 8, 2010. In 2016, Andrea and Kyle were residing in their own home in the West Portal neighborhood in San Francisco.

RUBIN, SANDRA JO (1947 –   )

Sandra Jo Rubin, wife of Gene V Glass, was born in Chicago on February 13, 1947, to Lawrence Rubin and Lorraine Ada Witz. Lawrence was a journeyman electrician, and Lorraine was a homemaker. Sandy's early years were spent in the Jewish neighborhoods of northwest Chicago: Logan Square & 1842 No. Humboldt Blvd. She attended Richard Yates Elementary School and Tuley High School through grade 10. She transferred to Niles West High School for grades 11 and 12 when her family moved to 5129 Fairview Lane in Skokie, Illinois.

Sandy's Rubin ancestral line goes back to Odessa, Ukraine. The descendants of Raphael Rubinovsky immigrated in 1905 to the Dayton, Ohio area. On her mother's side, she is a Witz and an Abraham, the Witz family having immigrated to Chicago from Riga, Latvia.

Sandy attended the University of Illinois – Chicago from 1964 to 1966. She graduated from the National College of Education in 1968. On August 18, 1968, she married Lawrence Charles Rosenthal, whom she had met through carpooling to college at UI.

Sandy's first teaching job was in the Evanston (IL) Public Schools at the junior high school level. The Vietnam War precipitated a decision on her husband Lawrence's part to enter the Public Health Service as a pharmacist. The couple was assigned to the Navajo Reservation in Shiprock, New Mexico, where they resided for three years. Sandy's daughter Michelle Ann was born on September 24, 1970, in Shiprock. Kyle Nathan Rosenthal was born on August 5, 1973, in Shiprock. Sandy spent those years raising her babies, making a home, and doing some substitute teaching.

Sandy and Larry moved to North Hollywood, California, in 1973, so that Larry could attend graduate school at the University of Southern California. In 1974, they faced a decision as to where to settle; they chose Phoenix, Arizona, because there was a position open for Larry at the Phoenix Indian Medical Center with the Public Health Service. They resided at 3032 West Hearn Road. Sandy had continued her graduate education while in Shiprock and North Hollywood, and eventually completed an Masters degree in the teaching of earth sciences at Northeastern (IL) University.

The couple divorced in 1976. Sandy taught school at Valley Jewish Day School in Phoenix for several years in the late 1970s and early 1980s, eventually attaining the position of Assistant Principal. She entered graduate school in the College of Education at Arizona State University. On June 7, 1981, she married Gerald Golner, a Phoenix pediatrician and founder of Phoenix Pediatrics. The couple resided at 1006 West Frier Drive in Phoenix until 1991, when they divorced.

Glass Family in America

Sandy enrolled in the PhD program in Educational Leadership & Policy Studies in 1989 at Arizona State University. She was awarded her degree in May, 1993. She married Gene V Glass on May 16, 1993, in Scottsdale, Arizona. In the 25 years between 1991 and 2016, she has split her time between Scottsdale, Arizona, and Boulder, Colorado. Sandy has been known professionally as Sandra Rubin Glass since the mid-1990s.

Michelle Ann (Rosenthal) Thompson, stepdaughter of Gene V Glass, was born on September 24, 1970, in Shiprock, New Mexico, to Sandra Jo Rubin and Lawrence Charles Rosenthal. She was their first child. She attended Valley Jewish Day School, Royal Palm Elementary School, Greenway High School, Ottawa University, and Arizona State University. She earned a Masters degree in reading instruction from Arizona State University in 2001. On November 7, 2004, she married **Justin John Thompson** of Eagar, Arizona. The couple was married in Tempe, Arizona. Justin is the son of John Thompson and Cherylann La Seuer of Eagar, Arizona,

and is a fourth generation descendant of John D. Lee. Michelle and Justin's son **Josdan Hayes Thompson** was born on August 11, 2005; he was born in Show Low, Arizona. **Jaytin Will Thompson** was born on February 15, 2007, in Show Low. Michelle has taught elementary school in Scottsdale, Heber, and Pima in Arizona, and in Dalhart and Hartley, Texas for twenty years. The Thompsons resided in Pima, Arizona, in 2016. Justin is employed as a Fire Management Officer by the U.S. Forest Service, Department of Agriculture.

Kyle Nathan Rosenthal, stepson of Gene V Glass, attended school at Valley Jewish Day School, Richard Miller Elementary, Royal Palm Jr. High, Sunnyslope, and Saguaro High Schools. He transferred from Scottsdale Community College to Arizona State University and completed a Bachelors degree in Business in 1998.

At age 6, Kyle contracted Acute Lymphocytic Leukemia. He was schedule for three years of chemotherapy, but after 18 months contracted Valley Fever[29] and had to be taken off of chemotherapy. Fortunately, his immune system fought off both illnesses, and he has enjoyed complete remission ever since.

Kyle moved to San Francisco shortly after college and worked in various technology companies before starting his own company, TachTech (www.tachtech.net) in the early 2000s. TachTech was honored in 2014 as one of the top 500 fast growing companies in the technology sector.

---

[29] Valley fever is a fungal infection caused by coccidioides organisms. It can cause fever, chest pain, and other more serious signs. It can result in a very serious infection, in some cases fatal.

Glass Family in America

Kyle married **Andrea Sayers**, an ASU business college graduate, on April 4, 2004, in Tempe, Arizona. Their daughter, **Bianca Lauren Rosenthal**, was born on February 8, 2010, in San Francisco. The family resides in their own home in the West Portal district of San Francisco.

In 1997, Sandy was reunited with a man whom she had given up for adoption at his birth on January 19, 1969. **Marc Zeidman** was located by searchers hired by Sandy's first husband, Lawrence Rosenthal. In 2016, Marc is living in Buffalo Grove, Illinois, with his wife **Rebecca and four sons: Jared, Michael, Zachary, and Ethan**. He is an electrical engineer working in the utilities industry and holds a Bachelors degree from the University of Kansas. Marc is, of course, a full sibling of Michelle (Rosenthal) Thompson and Kyle Nathan Rosenthal.

RYD, JAN (1959 –)

Jan Ryd, husband of Karen Sue Glass was born in Elgin, Illinois on April 15, 1959. Jan is the son of Inger Marie Halberg (born October 20, 1930) and Charles Gustov Ryd (born March 8, 1931, Brooklyn, New York). Both parents were raised in Kungsängen, Sweden. (Kungsängen is a city approximately 20 miles northwest of Stockholm; in 2010, its population was about 10,000 persons.) Jan's parents immigrated to the U.S. in 1955, though Charles had always maintained his U.S. citizenship. Inger died on March 16, 1990, of breast cancer. Jan was raised mostly in North Salem, New York, a suburb of New York City, approximately 50 miles north of Manhattan. Jan graduated high school in 1977. He moved to Colorado in June, 1978, and first found  employment as a cook at a restaurant in Littleton where Karen worked as a waitress. Jan worked as cook and assistant chef at a succession of restaurants in the Denver area, including Professor Plums, the Briarwood, the Denver Broker, the Coach House, El Rancho, and Jonathan's. He served as head chef at American Steak and Lobster.

Jan entered the business K's Cleaning Company that had been started by Karen in 1984. Both Karen and Jan ran the company until 2004 when they opened Lee Myles Autocare in Lakewood, Colorado. They operated both businesses until 2010 when they sold the cleaning business. In 2013, they opened Lee Myles Autocare in Northglen, Colorado, and in 2015, Lee Myles Autocare in Boulder, Colorado.

SABIN, MARY LOU (1933 –   )

Mary Lou Sabin, wife of Edwin Gordon Glass (Generation 13) was born in Lincoln, Nebraska, on May 5, 1933. She attended the elementary and secondary schools in Lincoln and graduated from Northeast High School in 1951. She married Edwin at St. Paul Methodist Church on August 10, 1951.

Mary Lou is the daughter of William Edward Sabin (born in 1885 in Smartville, Johnson County, Nebraska) and Mary Ann Estes (born in 1901 in Lincoln). Both of her parents were deaf, her father having lost his hearing from scarlet fever and meningitis at age 2 and her mother having been born deaf. Both parents were educated at the Nebraska School for the Deaf in Omaha, which was closed in 1998. William worked as a flooring and carpet installer. Mary Lou has two siblings: Betty, an older sister who lives in Scottsdale, Arizona, and Bill, a younger brother who lives in Lincoln, Nebraska. The Sabin line has been traced back to Richard Sabin who was born in Hampshire, England, in 1530. Mary Lou's Estes ancestors were known to have lived in Kentucky in the early 1800s.

SAWVEL, PIET MARK (1966 –   )

Piet Mark Sawvel is the husband of Julie Evann Glass. Piet was born on November 7, 1966, to Richard Keith Sawvel and Dorothy Conklin in Aspen, Colorado. He has three siblings: Dawn (Sawvel) Young, Pamela (Sawvel) Duffy, and Matthew Sawvel. He was raised in Montrose, Colorado, and Appleton, Wisconsin.

He was educated in both public and parochial schools in Appleton, and at the University of Colorado Boulder, where he completed a Bachelors degree in Journalism in 1990. Piet was employed for several years as a graphic designer at the *Colorado Daily*. More recently, he has served as a senior IT specialist at IBM since 2000; in 2016, his position was Digital Production Lead. In 2013, Piet served as a consultant in Malaysia as part of an IBM team to provide services to other nations.

Piet and Julie were married on May 28, 1995, in Boulder, Colorado. They have two children: Isaac Benjamin Sawvel and Eliana Rose Sawvel. Piet is an avid bicyclist and snowboarder, activities that he pursues around the world.

SHERMAN, HEATHER ELIZABETH (1981 -)

Heather Sherman was born on September 29, 1981, at Cedar Sinai Medical Center in Los Angeles. She is the daughter of Paul David Sherman and Carole Runcie Sherman. Heather attended Redwood Middle School and Thousand Oaks High School, where she graduated in May, 2000, in California. Heather was awarded a Bachelor of Science degree in Economics from the University of California, San Diego in May, 2004.

Heather married Jason Scott Glass on July 25, 2009, in Cozumel, Mexico. Heather and Jason have two children, as of April, 2016: Jackson Paul, born June 26, 2013, and Cameron Elizabeth, born April 12, 2016. Both children were born at Rose Medical Center in Denver, Colorado.

As of November, 2016, Heather has been employed for eight years by the medical device manufacturer Medtronic as a Project Manager in the area of Dialysis.

SMITH, MARY LEE (1944 –)

Mary Lee Smith was the second wife of Gene V Glass. They married on June 19, 1977, at their residence at 1735 Gillaspie Drive in Boulder, Colorado. Mary Lee was born on April 11, 1944, in Sioux Falls, South Dakota. She was placed for adoption at birth by her biological mother. She was adopted by Edwin R. and Eunice Carstens,

who settled in the Denver, Colorado, area on a farm in the vicinity of Sheridan and 88th Ave. In about 1950, the family moved to Dartmouth Avenue in Englewood, Colorado. Mary Lee attended Englewood High School, and entered the University of Colorado Boulder. She graduated in 1966 and after earning a Masters degree in Counseling, she worked for a time at CU Denver as a counselor. After high school and while attending college, she met and married Victor Smith, from whom she took the surname that she has used since.

Mary Lee Smith completed a PhD in Counseling at the University of Colorado in 1972. She divorced her second husband, Daniel Klingler, in 1974. She served on the faculty of the University of Colorado from 1977 until 1986, when both she and Gene accepted positions at Arizona State University in Tempe, Arizona. Mary Lee and Gene divorced in 1991.

During her professional career, she wrote several books and many articles in scholarly journals. Mary Lee was awarded the title of Regents' Professor by the Arizona Board of Regents in 2004, an honor reserved for 1% of the faculties at the three public universities in Arizona: Arizona State University, the University of Arizona, and Northern Arizona University.

She met James Robert (Jimmy) Shutt, a Viet Nam war veteran and Phoenix business owner in 1991. They lived together for 23 years, moving to Longmont, Colorado in 2010. They married in 2014. Within months of their marriage, Jimmy was diagnosed with Stage 4 lung cancer. He died on March 24, 2015, in Longmont. Mary Lee was residing in Longmont, Colorado, in 2016.

SPENCE, WARREN CLEMENTS (1926 – 2014)

Warren Clements Spence, husband of Ellen Gay Glass, was born on July 22, 1926, in Riverton, Nebraska, a very small town in central Nebraska on the border with Kansas. (In the 2010 Census, the population of Riverton was 89 persons.) His parents were Charles and Ellen (Clements) Spence. He graduated from Lincoln Northeast High

School in 1944. Warren was in the Army from 1944 to 1946. He served as a prison guard at a POW camp in Alabama. Warren started at the United States Postal Service in 1957 and retired in 1986, as a Postal Distribution Clerk. He was an avid sports fan who followed the Nebraska Cornhuskers, but he broke ties with them when ticket prices soared. He loved to listen to recorded opera music and had a large collection of vinyl records. He died before his 88th birthday on February 16, 2014, having been  treated for prostate cancer and non-Hodgkins lymphoma for many years. Warren is buried in Wyuka Cemetery in Lincoln, Nebraska.

SELECTED DESCENDANTS OF JOHN GLASSE OF TAUNTON, SOMERSET, ENGLAND

Recorded here are the basic biographical facts of some of the descendants of John Glasse, who was born in Taunton, Somerset, England, in 1561. The selection of which branches of the family tree were followed to construct this record was governed by two considerations: 1) persons with the surname Glass descending from the four siblings (Amy, James, Roger, Henry) who immigrated to Massachusetts in 1637; 2) persons whose descendants would be likely to be interested in this genealogical account.

GENERATION 1

JOHN GLASSE was born in 1561 in Taunton, Somerset, England. He died in 1590 in Taunton, Somerset, England. He married Johane Dixon on 06 Jul 1579 in Taunton, Somerset, England. She was born in 1561 in Taunton, Somerset, England. She died on 22 Feb 1639 in Taunton, Somerset, England.

John Glasse and Johane Dixon had the following children:

> HENRY GLASS was born in 1614 in Taunton, Somerset, England. He died in 1620 in Taunton, Somerset, England.
>
> MARY GLASS was born about 1617 in Taunton, Somerset, England. She died date Unknown.
>
> AMY GLASS was born in 1618 in Taunton, Somerset, England. Amy died in Jan 1648 in Massachusetts.
>
> JAMES GLASS was born about 1591 in Taunton, Somerset, England. He died on 22 Feb 1638 in Taunton,

Somerset, England. He married Mary Cogan on 24 Jun 1612 in Taunton, Somerset, England. She was born on 22 Nov 1595.

ROGER GLASS was born in 1623 in Taunton, Somerset, England. He died on 27 Aug 1692 in Duxbury, Plymouth, Massachusetts.

HENRY GLASS was born in 1624 in Taunton, Somerset, England. He died date Unknown.

JOAN GLASS was born about 1626 in Taunton, Somerset, England. She died in Jul 1627 in Taunton, Somerset, England.

JOANE GLASS was born in 1629 in Taunton, Somerset, England. She died in 1640 in Taunton, Somerset, England.

RICHARD GLASS was born in 1616 in Taunton, Somerset, England. He died in 1629 in Taunton, Somerset, England.

PETER GLASS was born in 1631 in Taunton, Somerset, England. He died in Aug 1637 in Taunton, Somerset, England.

THAMAZEN GLASS was born in 1634 in Taunton, Somerset, England. She died in 1637 in Taunton, Somerset, England.

GENERATION 2

JAMES GLASS (John Glasse) was born about 1591 in Taunton, Somerset, England. He died on 22 Feb 1638 in

Taunton, Somerset, England. He married Mary Cogan on 24 Jun 1612 in Taunton, Somerset, England. She was born on 22 Nov 1595.

James Glass and Mary Cogan had the following child:

>HENRY GLASS was born about 1624 in Taunton, Somerset, England.

GENERATION 3

HENRY GLASS (James, John Glasse) was born about 1624 in Taunton, Somerset, England.

Henry Glass had the following child:

>RICHARD GLASS was born in 1655 in Manchester, Essex, Massachusetts. He married ELIZABETH FOX. She was born about 1655.

GENERATION 4

RICHARD GLASS (Henry, James, John Glasse) was born in 1655 in Manchester, Essex, Massachusetts. He married ELIZABETH FOX. She was born about 1655.

Richard Glass and Elizabeth Fox had the following children:

>RICHARD GLASS was born on 15 Mar 1687 in Manchester, Essex, Massachusetts. He died on 28 Oct 1741 in Pemaquid, Lincoln, Maine. He married Elizabeth Curteis on 04 Mar 1712 in Marblehead, Essex, Massachusetts. She was born in 1691 in Essex, Massachusetts. She died in 1723.

MARY GLASS was born on 27 Oct 1684 in Marblehead, Essex, Massachusetts.

JOANE GLASS was born on 13 Nov 1686 in Marblehead, Essex, Massachusetts.

GENERATION 5

RICHARD GLASS (Richard Glass, Henry, James, John Glasse) was born on 15 Mar 1687 in Manchester, Essex, Massachusetts. He died on 28 Oct 1741 in Pemaquid, Lincoln, Maine. He married Elizabeth Curteis on 04 Mar 1712 in Marblehead, Essex, Massachusetts. She was born in 1691 in Essex, Massachusetts. She died in 1723.

Richard Glass and Elizabeth Curteis had the following children:

> ANTHONY RICHARD GLASS was born in 1719 in Manchester, Essex, Massachusetts. He died in 1780 in Canterbury, Windham, Connecticut. He married Eunice Bennett on 19 Jun 1740 in New London, Connecticut. She was born on 05 May 1721 in New London, Connecticut. She died in 1762 in Canterbury, Windham, Connecticut.

> STEPHEN GLASS was born in 1722 in Essex, Massachusetts. He died in 1780 in Canterbury, Windham, Connecticut.

> JAMES GLASS was born in 1718 in Marblehead, Essex, Massachusetts. He died in 1770 in Colchester, New London, Connecticut.

GENERATION 6

Glass Family in America

ANTHONY RICHARD GLASS (Richard Glass, Richard Glass, Henry, James, John Glasse) was born in 1719 in Manchester, Essex, Massachusetts. He died in 1780 in Canterbury, Windham, Connecticut. He married Eunice Bennett on 19 Jun 1740 in New London, Connecticut. She was born on 05 May 1721 in New London, Connecticut. She died in 1762 in Canterbury, Windham, Connecticut.

Anthony Richard Glass and Eunice Bennett had the following children:

> EUNICE GLASS was born on 28 Apr 1742 in Canterbury, Windham, Connecticut. She died on 16 Oct 1749 in Canterbury, Windham, Connecticut.
>
> LOIS GLASS was born on 01 Jan 1743 in Canterbury, Windham, Connecticut.
>
> JAMES GLASS was born on 31 May 1744 in Canterbury, Windham, Connecticut. He died in 1798. He married RUTH BASSETT. He married HANNAH SUFFORD.
>
> SILAS GLASS was born on 30 Aug 1746 in Canterbury, Windham, Connecticut.
>
> PRUDENCE GLASS was born on 08 Mar 1748 in Canterbury, Windham, Connecticut.
>
> SARAH GLASS was born on 20 Aug 1751 in Canterbury, Windham, Connecticut.
>
> MARY GLASS was born on 15 Jun 1753 in Canterbury, Windham, Connecticut.

RUFUS GLASS was born on 07 Apr 1755 in Canterbury, Windham, Connecticut.

SAMUEL GLASS was born on 01 Apr 1758 in Canterbury, Windham, Connecticut.

EUNICE GLASS was born on 10 Jan 1760 in Canterbury, Windham, Connecticut.

GENERATION 7

JAMES GLASS (Anthony Richard Glass, Richard Glass, Richard Glass, Henry, James, John Glasse) was born on 31 May 1744 in Canterbury, Windham, Connecticut. He died in 1798. He married RUTH BASSETT. He married HANNAH SUFFORD.

James Glass and Ruth Bassett had the following children:

> REUBEN GLASS was born in 1787 in Whitingham, Windham, Vermont. He married Anna Wells in 1808 in Amsterdam, Montgomery, New York. She was born on 27 Oct 1790.
>
> CYRENUS GLASS was born on 08 Dec 1773 in Goshen, Connecticut.
>
> HEMAN GLASS was born in 1775.
>
> SARAH GLASS was born in 1777.
>
> ERASTUS GLASS was born in 1782. He died in Apr 1841 in Bath, Steuben, New York.

James Glass and Hannah Sufford had the following children:

Glass Family in America

PARTHENIA GLASS was born on 23 Feb 1769 in Canterbury, Windham, Connecticut.

PHILETUS GLASS was born in 1771 in Vermont.

GENERATION 8

REUBEN GLASS (James Glass, Anthony Richard Glass, Richard Glass, Richard Glass, Henry, James, John Glasse) was born in 1787 in Whitingham, Windham, Vermont. He married Anna Wells in 1808 in Amsterdam, Montgomery, New York. She was born on 27 Oct 1790.

Reuben Glass and Anna Wells had the following children:

ZENAS W. GLASS was born in 1812 in Westford, Otsego, New York. He died in 1857 in Nankin, Wayne, Michigan. He married Sarah Jane Ferris on 13 Jan 1839 in Nankin, Wayne, Michigan. She was born on 22 Aug 1821 in Elizabethtown, Essex, New York. She died on 22 Aug 1821 in Lincoln, Lancaster, Nebraska.

ISAAC JAMES GLASS was born in 1823 in Bath, New York. He died on 12 Apr 1909 in Livonia, Wayne, Michigan.

HARRIET GLASS was born in 1814.

HANNAH ANN GLASS was born in Dec 1815.

ALMIRA GLASS was born in 1819.

JAMES GLASS was born on 10 Nov 1821. He died on 20 Apr 1848 in Nankin, Wayne, Michigan.

EDGAR M. GLASS was born in 1825 in Bath, New York. He died in 1839 in Nankin, Wayne, Michigan.

EMORY P. GLASS was born on 01 Aug 1828 in Bath, New York. He died on 20 Sep 1901 in Livonia, Wayne, Michigan.

SARAH MELISSA GLASS was born on 28 Nov 1830 in Bath, New York.

GENERATION 9

ZENAS W. GLASS (Reuben Glass, James Glass, Anthony Richard Glass, Richard Glass, Richard Glass, Henry, James, John Glasse) was born in 1812 in Westford, Otsego, New York. He died in 1857 in Nankin, Wayne, Michigan. He married Sarah Jane Ferris on 13 Jan 1839 in Nankin, Wayne, Michigan. She was born on 22 Aug 1821 in Elizabethtown, Essex, New York. She died on 22 Aug 1821 in Lincoln, Lancaster, Nebraska.

Zenas W. Glass and Sarah Jane Ferris had the following children:

>EDWIN ZENIS GLASS was born on 04 Apr 1857 in Nankin, Wayne, Michigan. He died on 05 Jan 1933 in Lincoln, Lancaster, Nebraska. He married Eveline Gillet on 23 Mar 1881 in Perrinsville, Michigan. She was born on 11 Jul 1858 in Nankin, Wayne, Michigan. She died on 28 Jul 1923 in Lincoln, Lancaster, Nebraska.

>ELLEN GLASS was born in 1840 in Nankin, Wayne, Michigan. She died on 16 Nov 1893 in Nankin, Wayne, Michigan.

CORNELIA GLASS was born in 1842 in Nankin, Wayne, Michigan.

MILTON C. GLASS was born in 1840 in Nankin, Wayne, Michigan. He died on 01 Mar 1865 in Baltimore, Baltimore, Maryland.

MARTHA ANN GLASS was born on 06 Feb 1842 in Nankin, Wayne, Michigan. She died on 27 Mar 1845 in Nankin, Wayne, Michigan.

REUBEN E. GLASS was born on 13 Nov 1846 in Nankin, Wayne, Michigan. He died on 11 Oct 1905 in Broken Bow, Custer, Nebraska.

SARAH GLASS was born on 07 Oct 1848 in Nankin, Wayne, Michigan.

GENERATION 10

EDWIN ZENIS GLASS (Zenas W. Glass, Reuben Glass, James Glass, Anthony Richard Glass, Richard Glass, Richard Glass, Henry, James, John Glasse) was born on 04 Apr 1857 in Nankin, Wayne, Michigan. He died on 05 Jan 1933 in Lincoln, Lancaster, Nebraska. He married Eveline Gillett on 23 Mar 1881 in Perrinsville, Michigan. She was born on 11 Jul 1858 in Nankin, Wayne, Michigan. She died on 28 Jul 1923 in Lincoln, Lancaster, Nebraska.

Edwin Zenis Glass and Eveline Gillett had the following child:

EDWIN ORIGEN GLASS. He married NORA ELLEN JONES.

GENERATION 11

EDWIN ORIGEN GLASS (Edwin Zenis Glass, Zenas W. Glass, Reuben Glass, James Glass, Anthony Richard Glass, Richard Glass, Richard Glass, Henry, James, John Glasse). He married NORA ELLEN JONES on November 25, 1908, in Perkins County, Nebraska.

Edwin Origen Glass and Nora Ellen Jones had the following children:

> EDWIN ORVILLE GLASS was born on 24 Aug 1909 in Grant, Perkins, Nebraska. He died on 13 Oct 1994 in Lincoln, Lancaster, Nebraska. He married Grace Virginia Lintt on 19 Dec 1929 in Lincoln, Lancaster, Nebraska. She was born on 16 Feb 1912 in Lincoln, Lancaster, Nebraska.
>
> MILTON COLLINS GLASS was born on 30 May 1911 in Grant, Perkins County, Nebraska. He died on 20 Oct 1968 in Alhambra, California. He married ELEANOR IDAMAE HILLIARD. She was born on 12 Jun 1920 in Lincoln, Lancaster, Nebraska.
>
> LYLE CALVIN GLASS was born on 20 Nov 1913 in Grant, Perkins, Nebraska. He died on 29 Mar 1996 in Ocklawaha, Florida. He married Blanche Davis in 1930. She was born on 24 Apr 1909. She died on 01 Aug 1992 in Ocklawaha, Florida.
>
> VICTOR BUREN GLASS. He married Gladys Annette Davis on 13 Oct 1947 in Lincoln, Nebraska. She was born on 05 Mar 1919 in Eckley, Yuma, Colorado. She died on 14 Jul 1993 in Covina, Los Angeles, California.
>
> GAYLAND WARREN GLASS was born on 20 Feb 1920 in Olney Springs, Crowley, Colorado. He died on 09 Jun 2005 in Castle Rock, Douglas, Colorado. He

married Helen Virginia Baerenbach on 24 Jun 1943 in Manhattan, New York, New York. She was born in 1922 in Manhattan, New York, New York. She died on 05 Jul 2016 in Parker, Douglas, Colorado.

EVA ANN GLASS was born on 10 Jun 1926 in Lincoln, Lancaster, Nebraska. She died on 28 Jun 1936 in Lincoln, Lancaster, Nebraska.

GENERATION 12

EDWIN ORVILLE GLASS (Edwin Origen Glass, Edwin Zenis Glass, Zenas W. Glass, Reuben Glass, James Glass, Anthony Richard Glass, Richard Glass, Richard Glass, Henry, James, John Glasse) was born on 24 Aug 1909 in Grant, Perkins, Nebraska. He died on 13 Oct 1994 in Lincoln, Lancaster, Nebraska. He married Grace Virginia Lintt on 19 Dec 1929 in Lincoln, Lancaster, Nebraska. She was born on 16 Feb 1912 in Lincoln, Lancaster, Nebraska.

Edwin Orville Glass and Grace Virginia Lintt had the following children:

EDWIN GORDON GLASS was born on 22 Oct 1932 in Lincoln, Lancaster, Nebraska. He married Mary Lou Sabin on 10 Aug 1951 in Lincoln, Lancaster, Nebraska. She was born on 05 May 1933 in Lincoln, Lancaster, Nebraska.

ELLEN GAY GLASS was born on 17 Oct 1938 in Lincoln, Lancaster, Nebraska. She married Warren Clement Spence on 25 Jun 1958 in North Platte, Lincoln, Nebraska. He was born on 22 Jul 1926 in Riverton, Franklin, Nebraska.

GENE V GLASS was born on 19 Jun 1940 in Lincoln, Lancaster, Nebraska. He married (1) SHARON LEA GROSSOEHME on 16 Aug 1959. He married (2) MARY LEE SMITH on 19 Jun 1977 in Boulder, Boulder, Colorado. She was born on 11 Apr 1944 in Sioux Falls, Lincoln, South Dakota. He married (3) SANDRA JO RUBIN on 16 May 1993 in Scottsdale, Maricopa, Arizona. She was born on 13 Feb 1947 in Chicago, Cook, Illinois.

MILTON COLLINS GLASS (Edwin Origen Glass, Edwin Zenis Glass, Zenas W. Glass, Reuben Glass, James Glass, Anthony Richard Glass, Richard Glass, Richard Glass, Henry, James, John Glasse) was born on 30 May 1911 in Grant, Perkins County, Nebraska. He died on 20 Oct 1968 in Alhambra, California. He married ELEANOR IDAMAE HILLIARD. She was born on 12 Jun 1920 in Lincoln, Lancaster, Nebraska.

Milton Collins Glass and Eleanor Idamae Hilliard had the following children:

>PHILIP ROY GLASS was born on 21 Oct 1942 in Alhambra, California. He married (1) WILMA J. WADE on 31 Dec 1966. He married (2) MALINDA S. MOULTON on 01 Sep 1973 in Covina, Los Angeles, California. He married (3) KAREN D. DAYLEY-BURNETT in 1980 in Utah. She was born on 29 Dec 1945 in Ogden, Utah.

>PAUL RAYMOND GLASS was born in 1947 in Alhambra, California. He married Therese Pauline Eldridge on 23 Oct 1971 in Covina, Los Angeles, California. She was born on 04 Apr 1952 in Edwards AFB, Kern, California.

GLENN RUSSELL GLASS was born on 30 Jan 1957 in Alhambra, California. He married Shelly Belinda Ratcliff in Jun 1980 in Calimesa, Riverside, California. She was born on 19 Jun 1964 in San Bernardino, California.

LYLE CALVIN GLASS (Edwin Origen Glass, Edwin Zenis Glass, Zenas W. Glass, Reuben Glass, James Glass, Anthony Richard Glass, Richard Glass, Richard Glass, Henry, James, John Glasse) was born on 20 Nov 1913 in Grant, Perkins, Nebraska. He died on 29 Mar 1996 in Ocklawaha, Florida. He married Blanche Davis in 1930. She was born on 24 Apr 1909. She died on 01 Aug 1992 in Ocklawaha, Florida.

Lyle Calvin Glass and Blanche Davis had the following child:

CLINT LYLE GLASS was born on 24 Apr 1965 in Florida. He married Karen Boehmer on 14 Oct 1989 in Ocala, Marion, Florida. She was born on 14 Jan 1966.

VICTOR BUREN GLASS (Edwin Origen Glass, Edwin Zenis Glass, Zenas W. Glass, Reuben Glass, James Glass, Anthony Richard Glass, Richard Glass, Richard Glass, Henry, James, John Glasse) was born in Sharon Springs, Kansas, on September 18, 1920. He married Gladys Annette Davis on 13 Oct 1947 in Lincoln, Nebraska. She was born on 05 Mar 1919 in Eckley, Yuma, Colorado. She died on 14 Jul 1993 in Covina, Los Angeles, California.

Victor Buren Glass and Gladys Annette Davis had the following children:

GARY DEAN GLASS was born on 05 Dec 1948 in Lincoln, Lancaster, Nebraska. He died on 13 Jul 1995 in Clearfield, Utah. He married Sharon A. Rasco on 09 Jun 1973 in Los Angeles, California.

VIRGINA ANN GLASS was born in 1950.

GAYLAND WARREN GLASS (Edwin Origen Glass, Edwin Zenis Glass, Zenas W. Glass, Reuben Glass, James Glass, Anthony Richard Glass, Richard Glass, Richard Glass, Henry, James, John Glasse) was born on 20 Feb 1920 in Olney Springs, Colorado. He married HELEN VIRGINIA BAERENBACH on 24 Jun 1943 in Manhattan, New York, New York.

EVA ANN GLASS (Edwin Origen Glass, Edwin Zenis Glass, Zenas W. Glass, Reuben Glass, James Glass, Anthony Richard Glass, Richard Glass, Richard Glass, Henry, James, John Glasse) was born on 10 Jun 1926 in Lincoln, Nebraska. She died on 28 Jun 1936 in Lincoln, Nebraska.

GENERATION 13

EDWIN GORDON GLASS (Edwin Orville Glass, Edwin Origen Glass, Edwin Zenis Glass, Zenas W. Glass, Reuben Glass, James Glass, Anthony Richard Glass, Richard Glass, Richard Glass, Henry, James, John Glasse) was born on 22 Oct 1932 in Lincoln, Lancaster, Nebraska. He married Mary Lou Sabin on 10 Aug 1951 in Lincoln, Lancaster, Nebraska. She was born on 05 May 1933 in Lincoln, Lancaster, Nebraska.

Edwin Gordon Glass and Mary Lou Sabin had the following children:

> GREGORY SCOTT GLASS was born on 27 Aug 1954 in Lincoln, Lancaster, Nebraska. He married LINDA BUCHHOLTZ. He married SUSAN MARTINEZ on October 12, 2001 in Honolulu.

> KAREN SUE GLASS was born on 16 Jun 1956 in Lincoln, Lancaster, Nebraska. She married JAN RYD. He was born on 15 Apr 1959 in Elgin, Cook, Illinois.
>
> ZACHARY ALAN GLASS was born on 18 Sep 1958 in Lincoln, Lancaster, Nebraska. He married Sandra Hughes in 1985 in Denver. She was born on 28 Sep 1957 in Cleveland, Cuyahoga, Ohio.

ELLEN GAY GLASS (Edwin Orville Glass, Edwin Origen Glass, Edwin Zenis Glass, Zenas W. Glass, Reuben Glass, James Glass, Anthony Richard Glass, Richard Glass, Richard Glass, Henry, James, John Glasse) was born on 17 Oct 1938 in Lincoln, Lancaster, Nebraska. She married Warren Clement Spence on 25 Jun 1958 in North Platte, Lincoln, Nebraska. He was born on 22 Jul 1926 in Riverton, Franklin, Nebraska.

Ellen Gay Glass and Warren Clement Spence had the following child:

> LEONARD DEAN SPENCE was born on 02 Apr 1959 in Lincoln, Lancaster, Nebraska. He married Eam Ath on 05 Apr 1997 in Lincoln, Lancaster, Nebraska. She was born on 13 Apr 1966 in Battambang, Cambodia.

GENE V GLASS (Edwin Orville Glass, Edwin Origen Glass, Edwin Zenis Glass, Zenas W. Glass, Reuben Glass, James Glass, Anthony Richard Glass, Richard Glass, Richard Glass, Henry, James, John Glasse) was born on 19 Jun 1940 in Lincoln, Lancaster, Nebraska. He married (1) SHARON LEA GROSSOEHME on 16 Aug 1959. He married (2) MARY LEE SMITH on 19 Jun 1977 in Boulder, Boulder, Colorado. She was born on 11 Apr 1944 in Sioux Falls, Lincoln, South Dakota. He married (3) SANDRA JO RUBIN on 16 May 1993 in Scottsdale, Maricopa, Arizona. She was born on 13 Feb 1947 in Chicago, Cook, Illinois.

Gene V Glass and Sharon Lea Grossoehme had the following child:

>JULIE EVANN GLASS was born on 18 Oct 1963 in Madison, Dane, Wisconsin. She married PIET MARK SAWVEL.

PHILIP ROY GLASS (Milton Collins Glass, Edwin Origen Glass, Edwin Zenis Glass, Zenas W. Glass, Reuben Glass, James Glass, Anthony Richard Glass, Richard Glass, Richard Glass, Henry, James, John Glasse) was born on 21 Oct 1942 in Alhambra, California. He married (1) WILMA J. WADE on 31 Dec 1966. He married (2) MALINDA S. MOULTON on 01 Sep 1973 in Covina, Los Angeles, California. He married (3) KAREN D. DAYLEY-BURNETT in 1980 in Utah. She was born on 29 Dec 1945 in Ogden, Utah.

Philip Roy Glass and Karen D. Dayley-Burnett had the following children:

>JASON C. GLASS was born on 02 Mar 1982 in La Verne, California.

>KATIE D. GLASS was born on 17 Jan 1987 in La Verne, California.

PAUL RAYMOND GLASS (Milton Collins Glass, Edwin Origen Glass, Edwin Zenis Glass, Zenas W. Glass, Reuben Glass, James Glass, Anthony Richard Glass, Richard Glass, Richard Glass, Henry, James, John Glasse) was born in 1947 in Alhambra, California. He married Therese Pauline Eldridge on 23 Oct 1971 in Covina, Los Angeles, California. She was born on 04 Apr 1952 in Edwards AFB, Kern, California.

Glass Family in America

Paul Raymond Glass and Therese Pauline Eldridge had the following children:

> AIMEE KATHLEEN GLASS was born on 02 Jul 1974 in Fontana, California. She married DARREN SCOTT RICHARDS.
>
> ANNE MARIE GLASS was born on 01 Jul 1976 in Fontana, California. She married Roland Douglas Hoover in 1999. He was born on 10 Feb 1976 in San Bernardino, California.

GLENN RUSSELL GLASS (Milton Collins Glass, Edwin Origen Glass, Edwin Zenis Glass, Zenas W. Glass, Reuben Glass, James Glass, Anthony Richard Glass, Richard Glass, Richard Glass, Henry, James, John Glasse) was born on 30 Jan 1957 in Alhambra, California. He married Shelly Belinda Ratcliff in Jun 1980 in Calimesa, Riverside, California. She was born on 19 Jun 1964 in San Bernardino, California.

Glenn Russell Glass and Shelly Belinda Ratcliff had the following child:

> SCOTT CHANDLER GLASS was born on 04 Mar 1987.

CLINT LYLE GLASS (Lyle Calvin Glass, Edwin Origen Glass, Edwin Zenis Glass, Zenas W. Glass, Reuben Glass, James Glass, Anthony Richard Glass, Richard Glass, Richard Glass, Henry, James, John Glasse) was born on 24 Apr 1965 in Florida. He married Karen Boehmer on 14 Oct 1989 in Ocala, Marion, Florida. She was born on 14 Jan 1966.

Clint Lyle Glass and Karen Boehmer had the following children:

KAYLIN GLASS was born on 03 Mar 1993 in Ocala, Marion, Florida. She married Eric Cornelison in 2015.

COLTON JOSHUA GLASS was born on 31 May 2007 in Florida.

GENERATION 14

GREGORY SCOTT GLASS (Edwin Gordon Glass, Edwin Orville Glass, Edwin Origen Glass, Edwin Zenis Glass, Zenas W. Glass, Reuben Glass, James Glass, Anthony Richard Glass, Richard Glass, Richard Glass, Henry, James, John) was born on 27 Aug 1954 in Lincoln, Lancaster, Nebraska. He married LINDA BUCHHOLTZ. He married SUSAN MARTINEZ.

Gregory Scott Glass and Linda Buchholtz had the following children:

> JASON SCOTT GLASS was born on 04 Dec 1978 in Denver, Colorado. He married Heather Elizabeth Sherman on 25 Jul 2009 in Cozumel, Mexico. She was born on 29 Sep 1981 in Los Angeles, Los Angeles, California.
>
> JOSHUA STEVEN GLASS was born on 07 Nov 1981 in Denver, Colorado.

KAREN SUE GLASS (Edwin Gordon Glass, Edwin Orville Glass, Edwin Origen Glass, Edwin Zenis Glass, Zenas W. Glass, Reuben Glass, James Glass, Anthony Richard Glass, Richard Glass, Richard Glass, Henry, James, John) was born on 16 Jun 1956 in Lincoln, Lancaster, Nebraska. She married

Glass Family in America

JAN RYD. He was born on 15 Apr 1959 in Elgin, Cook, Illinois.

Karen Sue Glass and Jan Ryd had the following children:

>AMANDA LYNN RYD was born on 16 Sep 1990 in Denver, Colorado.

>ERIK SABIN RYD was born on 29 Aug 1993 in Conifer, Jefferson, Colorado.

>AXEL GORDON RYD was born on 26 Aug 1997 in Lakewood, Jefferson, Colorado.

ZACHARY ALAN GLASS (Edwin Gordon Glass, Edwin Orville Glass, Edwin Origen Glass, Edwin Zenis Glass, Zenas W. Glass, Reuben Glass, James Glass, Anthony Richard Glass, Richard Glass, Richard Glass, Henry, James, John Glasse) was born on 18 Sep 1958 in Lincoln, Lancaster, Nebraska. He married Sandra Hughes in 1985 in Denver. She was born on 28 Sep 1957 in Cleveland, Cuyahoga, Ohio.

Zachary Alan Glass and Sandra Hughes had the following children:

>KYLE LEE GLASS was born on 08 Aug 1986 in Denver, Colorado.

>DANE ALAN GLASS was born on 08 Aug 1986 in Denver, Colorado.

LEONARD DEAN SPENCE (Ellen Gay Glass, Edwin Orville Glass, Edwin Origen Glass, Edwin Zenis Glass, Zenas W. Glass, Reuben Glass, James Glass, Anthony Richard Glass, Richard Glass, Richard Glass, Henry, James, John Glasse) was born on 02 Apr 1959 in Lincoln, Lancaster, Nebraska. He married Eam Ath on 05 Apr 1997 in Lincoln, Lancaster, Nebraska. She was born on 13 Apr 1966 in Battambang, Cambodia.

Leonard Dean Spence and Eam Ath had the following children:

> AMANDA DARA ATH-SPENCE was born on 22 Oct 1992 in Lincoln, Lancaster, Nebraska. She partnered with CHRISTOPHER WILLIAM JOSEPH GREGGS. He was born in 1992 in Lexington, Nebraska.
>
> CHARLES MATTHEW ATH-SPENCE was born on 04 Sep 1996 in Lincoln, Lancaster, Nebraska.

JULIE EVANN GLASS (Gene V Glass, Edwin Orville Glass, Edwin Origen Glass, Edwin Zenis Glass, Zenas W. Glass, Reuben Glass, James Glass, Anthony Richard Glass, Richard Glass, Richard Glass, Henry, James, John) was born on 18 Oct 1963 in Madison, Dane, Wisconsin. She married PIET MARK SAWVEL.

Julie Evann Glass and Piet Mark Sawvel had the following children:

> ISAAC BENJAMIN SAWVEL was born on 28 Apr 1997 in Boulder, Boulder, Colorado.
>
> ELIANA ROSE SAWVEL was born on 22 May 2001 in Boulder County, Colorado.

AIMEE KATHLEEN GLASS (Paul Raymond Glass, Milton Collins Glass, Edwin Origen Glass, Edwin Zenis Glass, Zenas W. Glass, Reuben Glass, James Glass, Anthony Richard Glass, Richard Glass, Richard Glass, Henry, James, John Glasse) was

Glass Family in America

born on 02 Jul 1974 in Fontana, California. She married DARREN SCOTT RICHARDS.

Aimee Kathleen Glass and Darren Scott Richards had the following children:

>JARRED MICHAEL RICHARDS was born on 17 Jul 1999.

>JADEN CHRISTOPHER RICHARDS was born on 29 Jul 2001.

>ETHAN JAMES RICHARDS was born on 29 Jan 2004.

>MATTHEW JOEL RICHARDS was born on 06 Nov 2007.

>SHANE JOSEPH RICHARDS was born on 13 Oct 2009.

ANNE MARIE GLASS (Paul Raymond Glass, Milton Collins Glass, Edwin Origen Glass, Edwin Zenis Glass, Zenas W. Glass, Reuben Glass, James Glass, Anthony Richard Glass, Richard Glass, Richard Glass, Henry, James, John Glasse) was born on 01 Jul 1976 in Fontana, California. She married Roland Douglas Hoover in 1999. He was born on 10 Feb 1976 in San Bernardino, California.

Anne Marie Glass and Roland Douglas Hoover had the following children:

>BRYAN ROLAND HOOVER was born on 16 Jan 2003 in Pontiac, Oakland, Michigan.

>TREVOR DAVID HOOVER was born on 31 Jan 2007 in Redlands, San Bernardino, California.

GENERATION 15

JASON SCOTT GLASS (Gregory Scott Glass, Edwin Gordon Glass, Edwin Orville Glass, Edwin Origen Glass, Edwin Zenis Glass, Zenas W. Glass, Reuben Glass, James Glass, Anthony Richard Glass, Richard Glass, Richard Glass, Henry, James, John Glasse) was born on 04 Dec 1978 in Denver, Colorado. He married Heather Elizabeth Sherman on 25 Jul 2009 in Cozumel, Mexico. She was born on 29 Sep 1981 in Los Angeles, Los Angeles, California.

Jason Scott Glass and Heather Elizabeth Sherman had the following children:

> JACKSON PAUL GLASS was born on 26 Jun 2013 in Denver, Colorado.

> CAMERON ELIZABETH GLASS was born on 12 Apr 2016 in Denver, Colorado.

AMANDA DARA ATH-SPENCE (Leonard Dean Spence, Ellen Gay Glass, Edwin Orville Glass, Edwin Origen Glass, Edwin Zenis Glass, Zenas W. Glass, Reuben Glass, James Glass, Anthony Richard Glass, Richard Glass, Richard Glass, Henry, James, John Glasse) was born on 22 Oct 1992 in Lincoln, Lancaster, Nebraska. She partnered with CHRISTOPHER WILLIAM JOSEPH GREGGS. He was born in 1992 in Lexington, Nebraska.

Amanda Dara Ath-Spence and Christopher William Joseph Greggs had the following children:

> CAYDIN WARREN GREGGS was born on 26 Oct 2010 in Lincoln, Lancaster, Nebraska.

MALEAH RENE GREGGS was born on 12 Dec 2014 in Lincoln, Lancaster, Nebraska.

REFERENCES

Some of the information about the four Glass siblings who immigrated from England in 1637 has been taken from a privately published genealogy: Shaver, Robert H. (1993) *From Great Britain to Western Illinois: A Glass-Cone-Smith Genealogical Sequel to Plant a Tree by Alan E. Shaver.* Bloomington, IN. Other references consulted include the following:

History of Wells, Vermont, for the First Century After Its Settlement. Cornell University Library.

History of the Town of Duxbury, Massachusetts: With Genealogical Registers, published in 1849 by Justin Winsor.

Morris, Larry E. (2000) Oliver Cowdery's Vermont years and the origins of Mormonism.
https://ojs.lib.byu.edu/spc/index.php/BYUStudies/article/viewFile/6631/6280

New England, The Great Migration and The Great Migration Begins, 1620 – 1635

Some Facts About the Early History of Whitingham Vermont. A. A. Butterfield. Published in 1916 by The Vermont Publishing Company of Brattleboro, Vermont.

The majority of the information reported in this account was obtained through Internet searches.

ACKNOWLEDGMENTS

The following persons contributed to the writing and publication of this account of the Glass family in America.

Paul and Teri Eldridge Glass of Yucaipa, California contributed information and photographs on the Milton Collins Glass family.

Edwin Gordon Glass and Ellen Gay (Glass) Spence contributed photographs and information on the Edwin Orville Glass family and its descendants.

Art Nehr and Doris Spehar of Long Island, New York contributed information and photographs on Gayland Warren Glass and his wife Helen Virginia Baerenbach.

My publisher, George Johnson, President of Information Age Publishing of Charlotte, North Carolina, graciously consented to usher the manuscript through the production process.

NAME INDEX

Indexed here are the names of certain principals among the descendants of John Glasse. Only those persons who were given a subheading (e.g., RICHARD GLASS, 1655 –   ; < Henry < James < John) have been indexed. A complete index of every name mentioned would have been prohibitively long.

Ath-Spence, Amanda Dara	109
Ath-Spence, Charles M.	109
Ath, Eam	115
Baerenbach, Helen Virginia	115
Boehmer, Karen	116
Buchholtz, Linda S.	116
Bumpas, Joseph	30
Bumpas, Rebecca	31
Cogan, Mary	117
Cornelison, Kaylin Nicole	103
Davis, Blanche	119
Davis, Gladys Annette	118
Eldridge, Therese Pauline	119
Ferris, Sarah	120
Frost, Claude T.	69
Frost, Kenneth Lyle	69
Frost, Milton David	59
Frost, Origen	124
Frost, Reuben Origen	59
Frost, Roderick Joseph	70
Frost, Roderick Paul	83
Frost, Sarah	56
Fuller, Huldah	119

Gillett, Eveline	....	124
Glass, Aimee Kathleen	....	102
Glass, Amy	....	17
Glass, Anne Marie	....	102
Glass, Anthony Richard	....	32
Glass, Cameron Elizabeth	....	114
Glass, Clint Lyle	....	96
Glass, Colton Joshua	....	104
Glass, Cyrenus	....	40
Glass, Dane Alan	....	108
Glass, Edwin Gordon	....	83
Glass, Edwin Origen	....	62
Glass, Edwin Orville	....	70
Glass, Edwin Zenis	....	57
Glass, Ellen Gay	....	85
Glass, Emory P.	....	50
Glass, Eva Ann	....	82
Glass, Gary Dean	....	96
Glass, Gene V	....	86
Glass, Glenn Russell	....	95
Glass, Gregory Scott	....	97
Glass, Hannah	....	24
Glass, Henry	....	23
Glass, Isaac James	....	49
Glass, Jackson Paul	....	114
Glass, James (1744 - 1798)	....	35
Glass, James (1590 - 1638)	....	14
Glass, James (1620 - 1652)	....	18
Glass, Jason Scott	....	104
Glass, Joshua Steven	....	105
Glass, Julie Evann	....	101
Glass, Karen Sue	....	98

Glass, Kyle Lee	....	108
Glass, Lyle Calvin	....	78
Glass, Milton C.	....	52
Glass, Milton Collins	....	77
Glass, Paul Raymond	....	90
Glass, Philetus	....	40
Glass, Philip Roy	....	89
Glass, Reuben	....	41
Glass, Reuben E.	....	54
Glass, Richard (Jr.)	....	31
Glass, Richard (Sr.)	....	25
Glass, Roger	....	19
Glass, Rufus	....	38
Glass, Samuel	....	34
Glass, Scott Chandler	....	103
Glass, Victor Buren	....	79
Glass, Virginia Ann	....	97
Glass, Warren Gayland	....	80
Glass, Wybra	....	23
Glass, Zachary Alan	....	99
Glass, Zenas W.	....	46
Glasse, John	....	14
Greggs, Caydin Warren	....	113
Greggs, Christopher	....	125
Greggs, Maleah Rene	....	114
Grossoehme, Sharon Lea	....	126
Hilliard, Eleanor Idamae	....	127
Hoover, Bryan Roland	....	112
Hoover, Roland Douglas	....	127
Hoover, Trevor David	....	113
Hughes, Sandra Lee	....	129

Hunt, Mary	....	24
Jones, Nora Ellen	....	129
Lintt, Grace Virginia	....	130
Martinez, Susan	....	131
Osband, Sarah Melissa	....	51
Pontus, Mary Elizabeth	....	134
Ratcliff, Shelly Belinda	....	135
Richards, Ethan James	....	111
Richards, Jaden Chistopher	....	111
Richards, Jarred Michael	....	111
Richards, Matthew Joel	....	111
Richards, Shane Joseph	....	111
Rosenthal, Andrea Diane	....	135
Rosenthal, Bianca Lauren	....	139
Rosenthal, Kyle Nathan	....	139
Rubin, Sandra Jo	....	136
Ryd, Amanda Lynn	....	106
Ryd, Axel Gordon	....	107
Ryd, Erik Sabin	....	107
Ryd, Jan	....	140
Sabin, Mary Lou	....	141
Sawvel, Eliana Rose	....	110
Sawvel, Isaac Benjamin	....	110
Sawvel, Piet Mark	....	142
Sherman, Heather Eliz.	....	143
Smith, Mary Lee	....	143
Spence, Leonard Dean	....	100
Spence, Warren Clements	....	144
Thompson, Michelle Ann	....	138
Tupper, Joseph	....	33
Willis, Richard	....	25
Willis, Ruhamah Ammi	....	29

Zeidman, Ethan	....	140
Zeidman, Jared	....	140
Zeidman, Marc	....	140
Zeidman, Michael	....	140
Zeidman, Rebecca	....	140
Zeidman, Zachary	....	140

www.ingramcontent.com/pod-product-compliance
Lightning Source LLC
Chambersburg PA
CBHW052100230426
43662CB00036B/1706